BEATTOCK TO CARSTAIRS

including the Moffat, Wanlockhead, Peebles (CR) and Dolphinton (CR) branch lines

Dennis Lovett

MP Middleton Press

Front cover: Class 92 no. 92017 approaches Crawford with the Tesco train heading north on 12th April 2010. It is working 4S43 the 06.25 from Daventry International Rail Freight Terminal (DIRFT) to the Direct Rail Services facility at Mossend. In addition to the Less CO2 branding the containers also carry a smaller TESCO logo as well as the Stobart logo, the logistics operator. (P.J.Robinson)

Back cover, upper: On 5th September 2004, Virgin Trains commissioned legendary railway photographer Colin Garratt to ascend 60ft into the air on a hired hydraulic platform to capture this picture during testing. With the line under possession for a simulated rescue, class 390 Pendolino no. 390049 successfully dragged no. 390021 dead from a standing start at 70mph over the steep incline. Floodlights were strung for a quarter of a mile, alongside the loop at Beattock, to ensure that the iconic picture was achieved. (C.Garratt/Milepost 92½/Transport Treasury)

Back cover, lower: Railway Clearing House map (edited), dated 1947. The route of the album is shown with a dotted line. The branch line to Wanlockhead, that closed in 1939, has been added.

ACKNOWLEDGEMENTS

We are grateful for the assistance received from many of those mentioned in the photographic credits and to D. Coddington, K. Darroch (Leadhills & Wanlockhead Railway), G. Croughton, R. R. Darsley, G. Gartside, C. Howard, N. Langridge, A. P. McLean, G. W. Morrison, D. & Dr S. Salter, M. Stewart (tickets), J. P. Vickers and J. W. Yellowlees (ScotRail).

Readers of this book may be interested in the following societies:

Caledonian Railway Association
https://www.crassoc.org.uk

Stephenson Locomotive Society
https://www.stephensonloco.org.uk

Leadhills & Wanlockhead Railway
https://leadhillsrailway.co.uk

Published February 2024

ISBN 978 1 910356 84 5

© *Middleton Press Ltd, 2024*

Cover design and Photographic enhancement Deborah Esher
Design & Production Cassandra Morgan

Published by
    Middleton Press Ltd
    Camelsdale Road
    Haslemere
    Surrey
    GU27 3RJ
Tel: 01730 813169
Email: info@middletonpress.co.uk
www.middletonpress.co.uk

Printed and bound by CPI Group (UK) Ltd, Croydon, CR0 4YY

SECTIONS

1.	Beattock to Carstairs (West Coast Main Line)	1-72	3.	Elvanfoot to Wanlockhead	77-84
			4.	Symington to Peebles (CR)	85-110
2.	Beattock to Moffat	73-76	5.	Carstairs to Dolphinton (CR)	111-120

CONTENTS

28	Abington	24	Crawford	73	Moffat
13	Auchencastle	118	Dolphinton CR	112	Newbigging
111	Bankhead	114	Dunsyre	105	Peebles CR/West
1	Beattock	20	Elvanfoot	14	Ruttonside
17	Beattock Summit	82	Glengonnar Halt	100	Stobo
90	Biggar	15	Greskine	37	Symington
95	Broughton	33	Lamington	44	Thankerton
54	Carstairs	79	Leadhills	99	Victoria Lodge
86	Coulter	102	Lyne	83	Wanlockhead

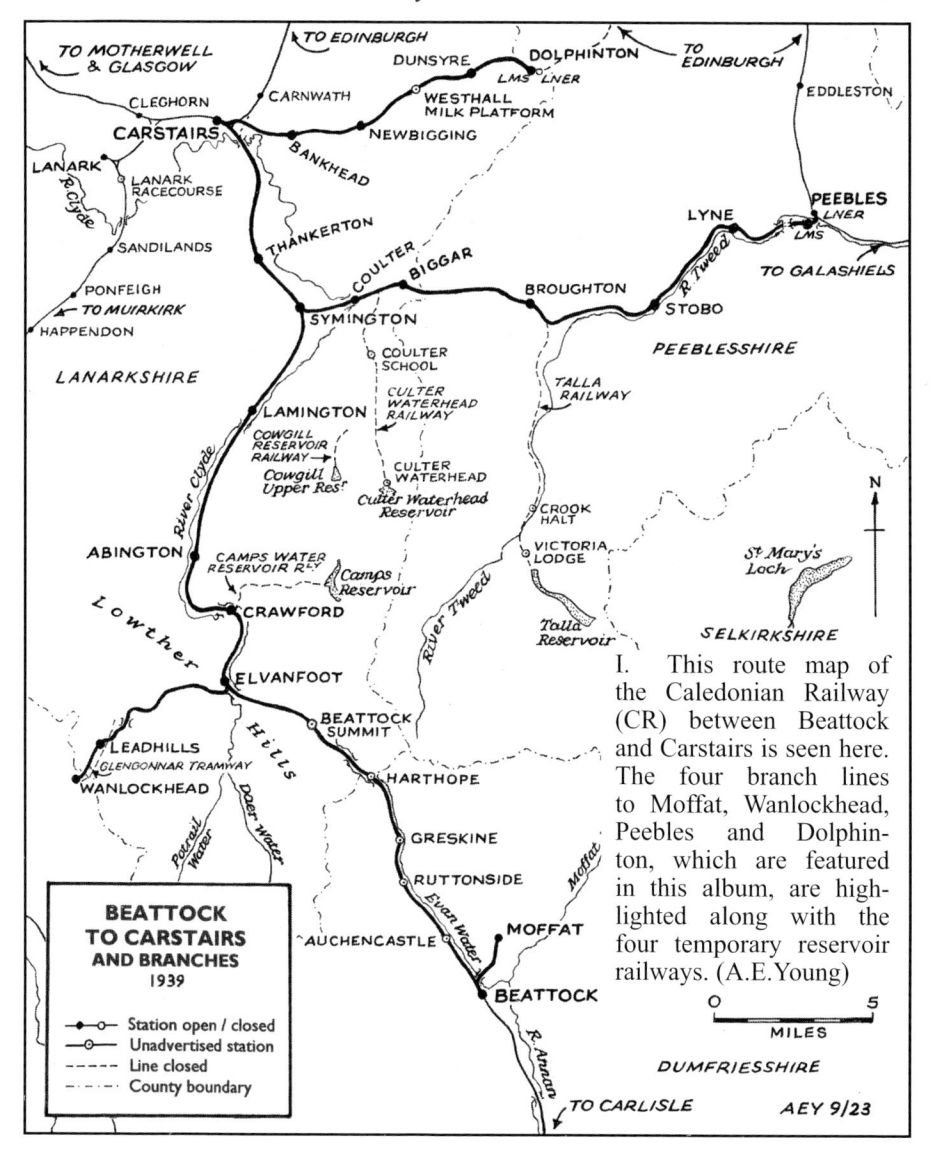

I. This route map of the Caledonian Railway (CR) between Beattock and Carstairs is seen here. The four branch lines to Moffat, Wanlockhead, Peebles and Dolphinton, which are featured in this album, are highlighted along with the four temporary reservoir railways. (A.E.Young)

GEOGRAPHICAL SETTING

The geography of the Scottish Borders provided three natural valley passages which could accommodate lines north of Carlisle to link it with the two largest Scottish cities of Edinburgh and Glasgow. The Caledonian Railway (CR) chose the line through Annandale to reach Beattock.

North of Beattock provided the railway with some difficult terrain. Beyond Beattock, the line starts to climb into the Lowther Hills, which form part of the Southern Uplands that lie to the west of the line. The Lowther Hills are composed of resistant Ordovician shales and provided employment by the mining of lead, silver and gold. Initially it follows the valley of the Evan Water before climbing to Beattock Summit, some 10 miles north of the former Beattock station to reach 1,016ft above sea level.

Beyond the Summit, the line drops down to the Clyde Valley following the course of the River Clyde from Elvanfoot to near Carstairs. To the east lie the Tweedsmuir hills and beyond Peebles the Moorfoot hills.

Much of the local industry is agricultural with sheep and cattle farming being prominent. This enabled wool to be supplied to the various mills in the Scottish Border towns such as Moffat, Peebles and further afield. Cattle was also a source of traffic with abattoirs at both Biggar and Broughton providing meat for onward transit to Smithfield Market, London.

Not surprisingly the area contains several reservoirs, four of which were constructed by supplies being carried on four temporarily laid railway lines.

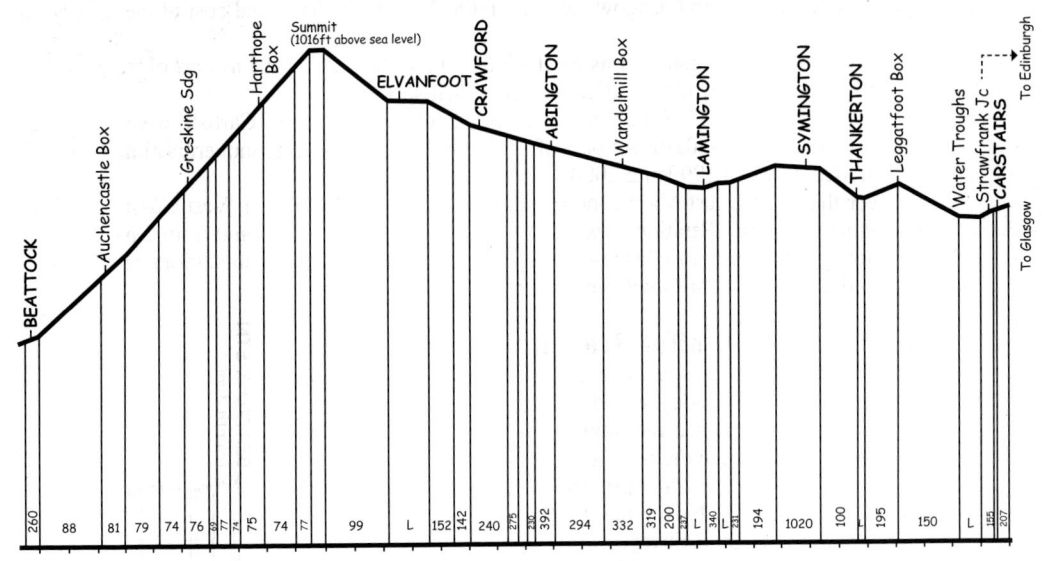

Gradient profile of the main line between Beattock and Carstairs. (Middleton Press)

HISTORICAL BACKGROUND

Plans to link Scotland with Carlisle were first discussed as early as 1835 although the government-appointed commissioners opted for the East Coast route via Berwick. The promoters of the alternative West Coast route did not give up and the Caledonian Railway received the Royal Assent on 31st July 1845 to build a line from Glasgow and Edinburgh, which joined up at Carstairs and thence to Carlisle.

The opening of the first section between Carlisle and Beattock took place on 10th September 1847. The section of line covered in this album was opened to traffic on 15th February 1848 along with the lines onwards to Glasgow and Edinburgh.

The Glasgow line north of Carstairs terminated at Garriongill, where it formed a junction with the Wishaw & Coltness Railway which, together with the lines of the Glasgow, Garnkirk & Coatbridge Railway (GG&CR), reached Glasgow, the first trains from Carlisle terminating at their Townhead terminus. From 1849 they used the inconvenient terminus South Side, which was already in use by the Glasgow, Barrhead and Neilston Direct Railway, for a short period. The Caledonian Railway then moved to the north of the city to use its own Buchanan Street terminus by building a new line from Milton Junction (opened 1st November 1849) off the Townhead line. These lines did not remain independent for long, the Wishaw & Coltness becoming part of the Caledonian in 1849 and the GG&CR was leased by the Caledonian in January 1846. The latter was originally a 4ft 6in gauge railway but was converted in August 1847 to standard gauge. The final act of amalgamation took place in June 1865, the GG&CR becoming part of the Caledonian. Services from Carlisle through Beattock and Carstairs were transferred to Glasgow Central on its opening in 1879.

The Edinburgh line originally terminated at Lothian Road. After the opening of Princes Street on 17th May 1847, Lothian Road became a goods station.

The main lines soon became part of the West Coast operation with trains being worked by the London & North Western Railway to Carlisle and from Carlisle north by the Caledonian Railway. Local services from Carlisle to Beattock were the domain of the Caledonian as were the freight workings.

On 1st January 1923 the London & North Western Railway and the Caledonian Railway both became part of the London, Midland & Scottish Railway at the Grouping. On nationalisation, on 1st January 1948, railways in Scotland became part of British Railways Scottish Region. The line between Carlisle and Gretna transferred to the London Midland Region.

Following the end of steam traction on British Rail in August 1968, diesels worked services until electrification of the 235-mile section of the West Coast Main Line from Weaver Junction (north of Crewe) to Motherwell. Authorised on 23rd February 1970 the new 'Electric Scots' services began operating throughout from London Euston to Glasgow Central on 6th May 1974. The final cost of the scheme was £74m.

The Edinburgh line from Carstairs was electrified from 18th March 1991 as part of the East Coast Main Line scheme championed by the InterCity sector of British Rail.

Following privatisation in 1997, express services on the route north of Carlisle were operated by Virgin Trains West Coast (1997-2019). As part of the West Coast Main Line modernisation programme the route was upgraded between 1999 and 2004.

Services over the West Coast Main Line are currently operated by Avanti West Coast, Caledonian Sleeper, CrossCountry and TransPennine Express. ScotRail provides services to and from Carstairs, which is served by Edinburgh Waverley to Glasgow Central trains. Today, there are no stations remaining that serve the communities on the 48 miles between Lockerbie and Carstairs.

The Moffat Branch

Moffat had developed as a spa town by 1878 when a hydropathic establishment opened which made use of the thermal springs there. The Caledonian main line by-passed the town, so it was left to the independent Moffat Railway to promote the line. Incorporated on 27th June 1881, the 1 mile 71 chain line opened on 2nd April 1883 and was worked from the onset by the Caledonian. On 1st November 1889, the Caledonian Railway absorbed the independent Moffat Railway.

The line was closed to passenger traffic on 6th December 1954 although its last passenger working was the Scottish Rambler Rail Tour on 29th March 1964. The line closed to freight shortly afterwards on 6th April 1964.

→ Gradient profile of the Moffat branch. (Middleton Press)

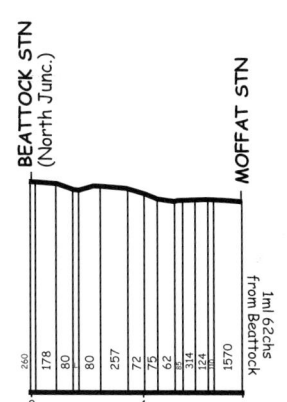

The Wanlockhead Branch

The Lowther Hills to the west of the main line were rich in mineral deposits of lead, silver and gold, which has been mined in the area for centuries. The mine owners had tried to interest the Caledonian Railway in building a line to serve them, but this was not achieved until the passing of the Light Railways Act in 1896. The passing of the act enabled rural railways to build to less demanding standards for which lower speed and weight limits were set. The line was not fenced and level crossings were ungated.

The standard gauge Leadhills & Wanlockhead Light Railway was authorised in 1898 and backed by the Caledonian. Construction of the 7¼ mile long line from a junction at Elvanfoot was carried out by Robert McAlpine Ltd. The largest structure was the Risping Cleuch viaduct which consisted of eight arches built in concrete and faced with bricks. It opened to Leadhills on 1st October 1901 and to Wanlockhead on 1st October 1902. Wanlockhead was the highest village in Scotland at 1,148ft above sea level and

Leadhills the second highest. The line was the highest adhesion worked line in the UK with only the rack and pinion line up Snowdon being higher.

A network of narrow-gauge lines linked the mines and smelters at Leadhills and Wanlockhead, one of which was the Glengonnar Tramway. This was a 2ft gauge system that was built around 1865 and pre-dated the railway by over 30 years. The narrow-gauge line was crossed by the Caledonian Railway by a flat crossing which was protected by gates in favour of the narrow-gauge line. The gates had to be closed to allow Caledonian trains to cross it. The Glengonnar line was horse-worked until 1922 when a battery electric loco was obtained from English Electric. By 1928 the smelter was closed, and the mines followed by 1931. There was a brief reopening in 1934 but soon afterwards they closed forever. With the decline in mining came a fall in population and the railway closed to all traffic on 2nd January 1939. The viaduct survived until 1991 when it was demolished.

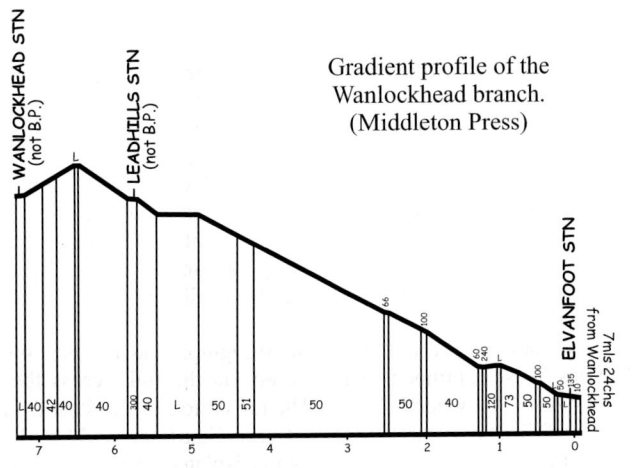

In 1986 a 2ft narrow gauge railway opened on the formation of the former standard gauge line between Leadhills and Glengonnar Halt towards Wanlockhead. The line is three quarters of a mile in length and operates as a heritage line on selected Sundays each Summer. Extension of the line to Wanlockhead is now in progress.

The Peebles Branch

The Caledonian Railway had identified Peebles for its plan to build a line from Glasgow towards Berwick. However, these plans, conceived in 1847, never came to fruition and it was left to the independent Peebles Railway to build a line from the county town to the north where it joined with the North British Railway's Hawick branch to enter Edinburgh.

Although it was an independent concern, the Symington, Biggar & Broughton Railway was backed by the Caledonian Railway which was authorised on 21st May 1858. The line between Symington and Broughton officially opened on 5th November 1860, and to public services the following day, although by then the Act of Parliament to extend the line to Peebles had already been obtained on 3rd July of that year. Amalgamation of the two companies took place in August 1861. Trains began running over the Broughton to Peebles section from 1st February 1864.

The Caledonian Railway and the North British Railway (NBR) were fierce rivals. Much of the Central and Eastern Borders was in the hands of the latter and the Caledonian Railway set its sights on penetrating into their rival's strongholds, which included the Midlothian coal field. The North British promoted the extension of the Peebles Railway to Galashiels via Innerleithen and this thwarted the Caledonian's threat of reaching the central and eastern Border towns with a projected line to Berwick. The line between Galashiels and Peebles opened on 1st October 1864, six months after the Caledonian had reached Peebles.

The NBR line to Peebles and Dolphinton is covered in our *Peebles Loop* album.

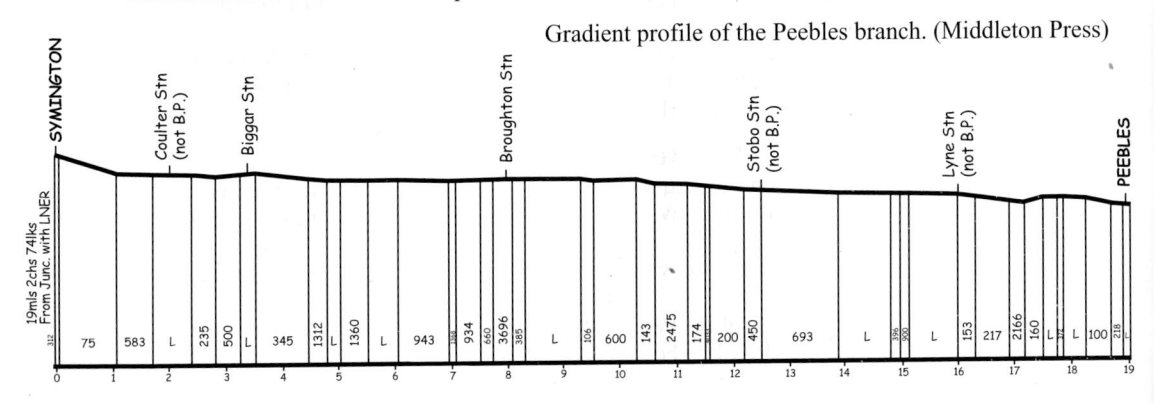

A link across the River Tweed at Peebles was opened on 16th April 1866, owned by the NBR, to provide the Caledonian access to the North British system and vice-versa. This was a government requirement as part of the authorisation to build the NBR line from Galashiels to Peebles.

Passenger services between Symington and Peebles continued following nationalisation in 1948 and closures of lightly used routes in Scotland were seeing their passenger services withdrawn although in many cases freight traffic continued. The last train departed the former Caledonian station at Peebles at 8pm on Saturday 3rd June 1950, the station officially closing to passengers on and from, Monday, 5th June 1950. The station remained open for goods and following the renaming of the former North British station to Peebles East in September 1952, ironically the now closed (to passenger traffic) CR facility became Peebles West!

Closure of the line between Broughton and Peebles West took place on 7th June 1954 although Peebles West continued to be served via the link across the Tweed from the North British line until 1st August 1959 when it closed. The rails into Peebles East from Peebles West were removed during 1961 and the following year services between Galashiels and Edinburgh via Peebles were withdrawn. By June 1963, the town of Peebles was totally isolated from the rail network. The line between Symington and Broughton closed to goods and completely on and from Monday, 4th April 1966.

The Dolphinton Branch

Just as the North British had blocked the route beyond Peebles, it was now the turn of the Caledonian to ensure that its rivals were kept out of the industrial towns of Lanarkshire by building a line from Carstairs to Dolphinton, which had been reached in 1864 by the Leadburn, Linton & Dolphinton Railway. This was taken over by the North British company two years later.

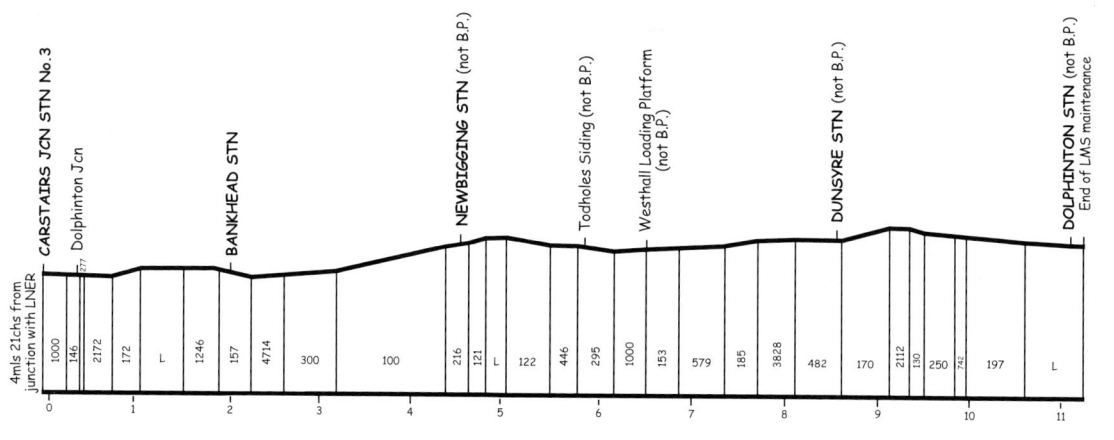

Gradient profile of the Dolphinton branch. (Middleton Press)

On 11th May 1863, the CR received the Royal Assent to build a line from Carstairs to Dolphinton. It is ironic that Scotland's two largest railway companies battled to serve a community that had a population of some 260. The result was two stations just 24 chains apart which were linked to allow the forwarding of goods trains from one company to another.

The CR line lost its passenger services on and from Monday, 4th June 1945 (the last trains running on Saturday, 2nd June) although it remained open for goods traffic until 1st November 1950. The North British line was closed to all traffic much earlier on 1st April 1933.

The Reservoir Railways

These were major construction sites requiring the transhipment of puddle clay and materials to build dams which took several years to construct. Workers trains were often run to enable the workforce to reach the site.

Three reservoirs were built to supply water to major conurbations in Lanarkshire and the fourth to supply Edinburgh.

Three of these lines were south of the Peebles branch whilst the other was served from Crawford on the main line. These lines are detailed elsewhere in this album.

PASSENGER SERVICES

Main Line
Beattock became the first station to open with the line from Carlisle on 10th September 1847. Through trains north of Beattock to Edinburgh and Glasgow via Carstairs began running on 15th February 1848. Intermediate stations were opened initially at Elvanfooot, Abington, Lamington, Symington and Thankerton.

Moffat branch
On opening, the line had some 15 trains a day in each direction. Between 1926 and 1948 services were worked by a former London & North Western Railway steam railcar. Journey time was between four and six minutes. The last timetable issued by the LMS in 1947 shows 15 workings in each direction on weekdays, which were reduced to 14 on Saturdays. There was no Sunday service.

Wanlockhead Branch
At closure there were four trains a day in operation in each direction. No trains ran on Sundays.

Peebles Branch
The opening of the line beyond Broughton to Peebles in 1864 saw an initial three trains a day which was soon increased to four in each direction. The journey time was around 45 minutes.

Later some trains ran to and from Carstairs with the number of trains increased to five on Saturdays.

The key business train of the day 'The Tinto Express', introduced before the outbreak of World War I, was named after Tinto Hill near Symington. Leaving Peebles at 7.45am its separate portions for Glasgow and Edinburgh reached their respective destinations at 9.30am. The Moffat coaches were attached at Symington. The return working left Edinburgh Princes Street at 4.45pm and Glasgow Central at 5pm. The Moffat portion was detached at Symington with Peebles being reached at 6.46pm.

The Edinburgh service from Peebles attempted to compete with the more direct route from the North British station at Peebles. A passenger leaving Peebles NBR at 8.00am would have been at Waverley before 9.00am. 'The Tinto Express' did however provide a faster journey to Glasgow than that of its NBR rivals.

Although no longer a named train, the early morning departure still ran into British Railways days. Passenger services on the branch were withdrawn on and from Monday, 5th June 1950.

Dolphinton Branch
The 1922 timetable shows three trains in each direction. There was no Sunday service.

↓ The Summer 1960 timetable shows stations between Beattock and Carstairs still being served by local trains. Most would be closed by the mid-1960s and the remaining branch lines used for goods traffic would also have disappeared. Today only Carstairs remains a timetable entry for the area covered by this album.

1. Beattock to Carstairs
BEATTOCK

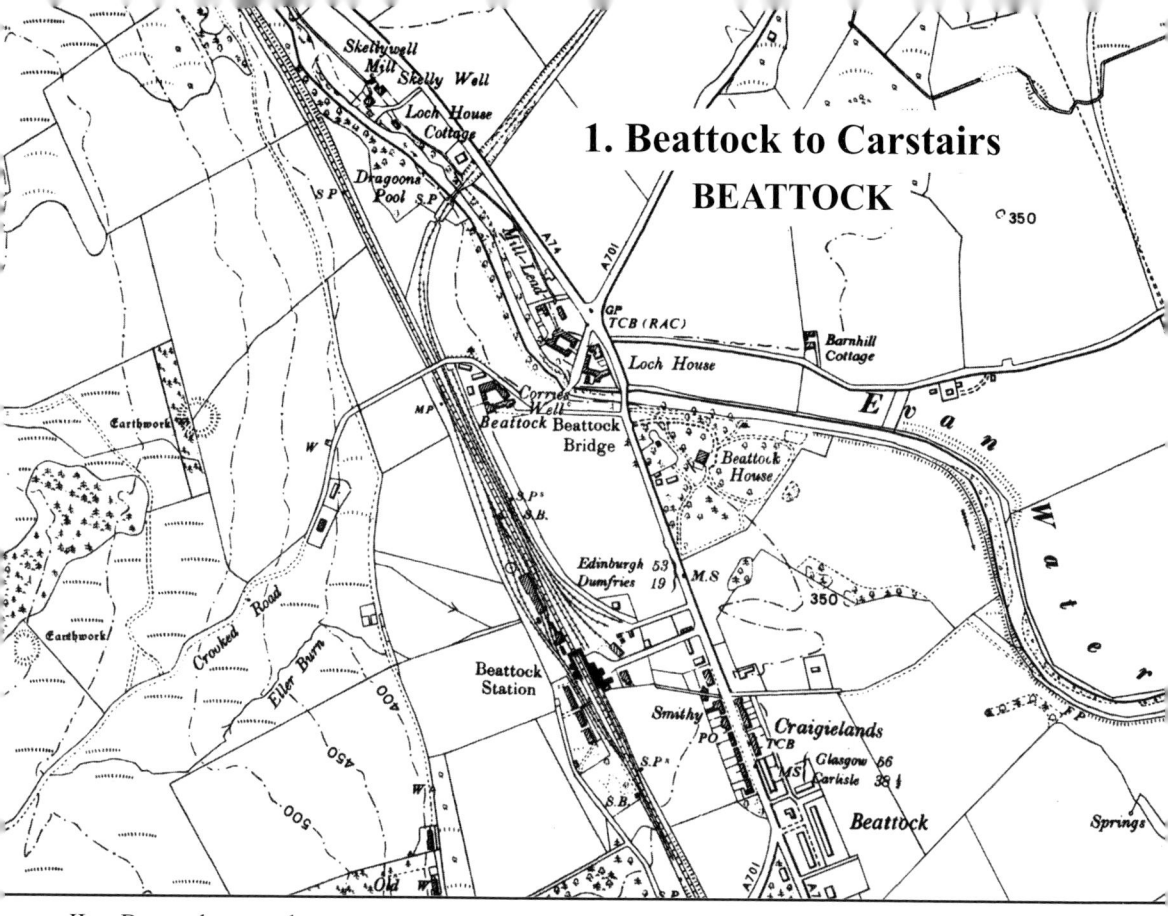

II. Beattock opened to passengers on 10th September 1847, the station building being designed by William Tite who was also responsible for Carlisle station amongst others. This 6in map dating from 1957 shows the Moffat branch heading off at the top of the picture to the right of the main line. The station closed to passengers on 3rd January 1972 and in recent years there has been a campaign to see it reopened for passenger traffic. Their plans were rejected by Transport Scotland in July 2023 and reopening is now highly unlikely.

1. The main station building viewed from the approach road. The cars on view date this as having been taken during the late 1950s or early 1960s. (N.Forrest/Transport Treasury)

2. A London & North Western Railway railmotor stands in the bay platform with a Moffat train on 2nd May 1948 whilst LMS Black 5 no. 4925 approaches with a goods train. (R.M.Casserley)

3. A view looking north of the impressive main building which was located on the up (southbound) platform and seen here in the late 1950s. (J.Mann/A.E.Young coll.)

4.   The driver of Kingmoor-allocated Black 5 4-6-0 no. 44900 has decided he has no need for a banker with 9 coaches in tow as he passes through Beattock with a northbound train on 20th May 1960. The station and engine shed in the background have been obliterated by smoke from the locomotive. (G.W.Morrison)

5.   No. 45613 *Kenya*, one of Stanier's Jubilee class 4-6-0s, works the 9.20am Morecambe to Glasgow relief service on 4th August 1962. A young trainspotter records the locomotive number in his notebook whilst a brake van sits at the buffer stops on the former Moffat branch platform. (W.A.C.Smith/Transport Treasury)

6. BR Standard 4MT 2-6-4T no. 80001 is on banking duties on 29th March 1964 giving assistance to the 09.30 Manchester to Glasgow Central as it heads past Beattock North box enroute to the Summit. (K.A.Gray/B.McCartney coll.)

7. Although the station had lost its passenger services two years earlier, the goods yard remained active when viewed from a passing train in 1974. The former Moffat bay platform can be seen to the left of the train and the station building has yet to be demolished. (W.Roberton)

Beattock Engine Shed

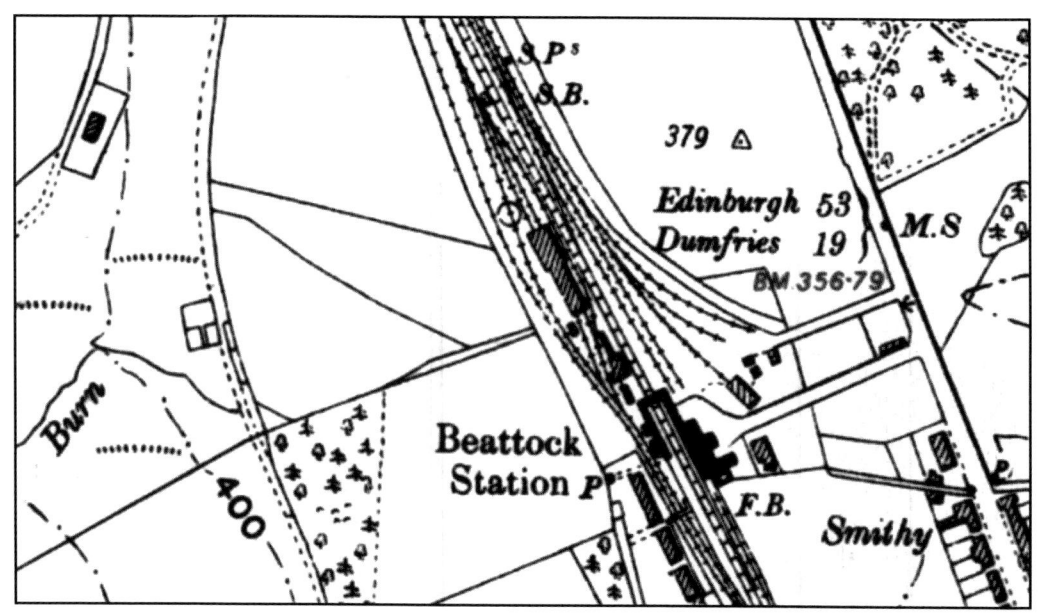

III. A 6in. map dated 1957 showing the steam shed north of the station. A facility was opened here in September 1847. In LMS days the depot was coded 12F under the former Caledonian Railway Kingmoor (Carlisle) shed. Initially a 42ft turntable was provided but this was replaced by a 54ft version in 1899. From 1st January 1949 until 30th June 1962, its locomotives carried a 68D shedcode. The shed then transferred to the Scottish Region under the control of Polmadie (Glasgow) as 66F until its closure to steam traction on 29th April 1967. It was replaced by a diesel stabling point (code BP) until it too closed on 30th November 1976, by which time most traffic was in the hands of electric locomotives. The shed building was finally demolished in 1978.

8. Fairburn 2-6-4T nos 42214 and 42239 pose outside the north end of the shed on 4th August 1962 whilst awaiting their next banking duties. (W.A.C.Smith/Transport Treasury)

9. Lonely looking McIntosh 3F 0-6-0 no. 57568 stands alongside the west wall of Beattock shed in March 1964. The ex-Caledonian Railway veteran had officially been withdrawn from Motherwell Shed (66B) at the end of 1963. (K.A.Gray/B.McCartney coll.)

Further pictures of Beattock and its shed can be found in our *Carlisle to Beattock* album.

10. On its very last day as a steam shed, BR Standard class 4MT 2-6-0 no. 76104 is being coaled on 29th April 1967. (W.A.C.Smith/Transport Treasury)

Moffat Branch Junction

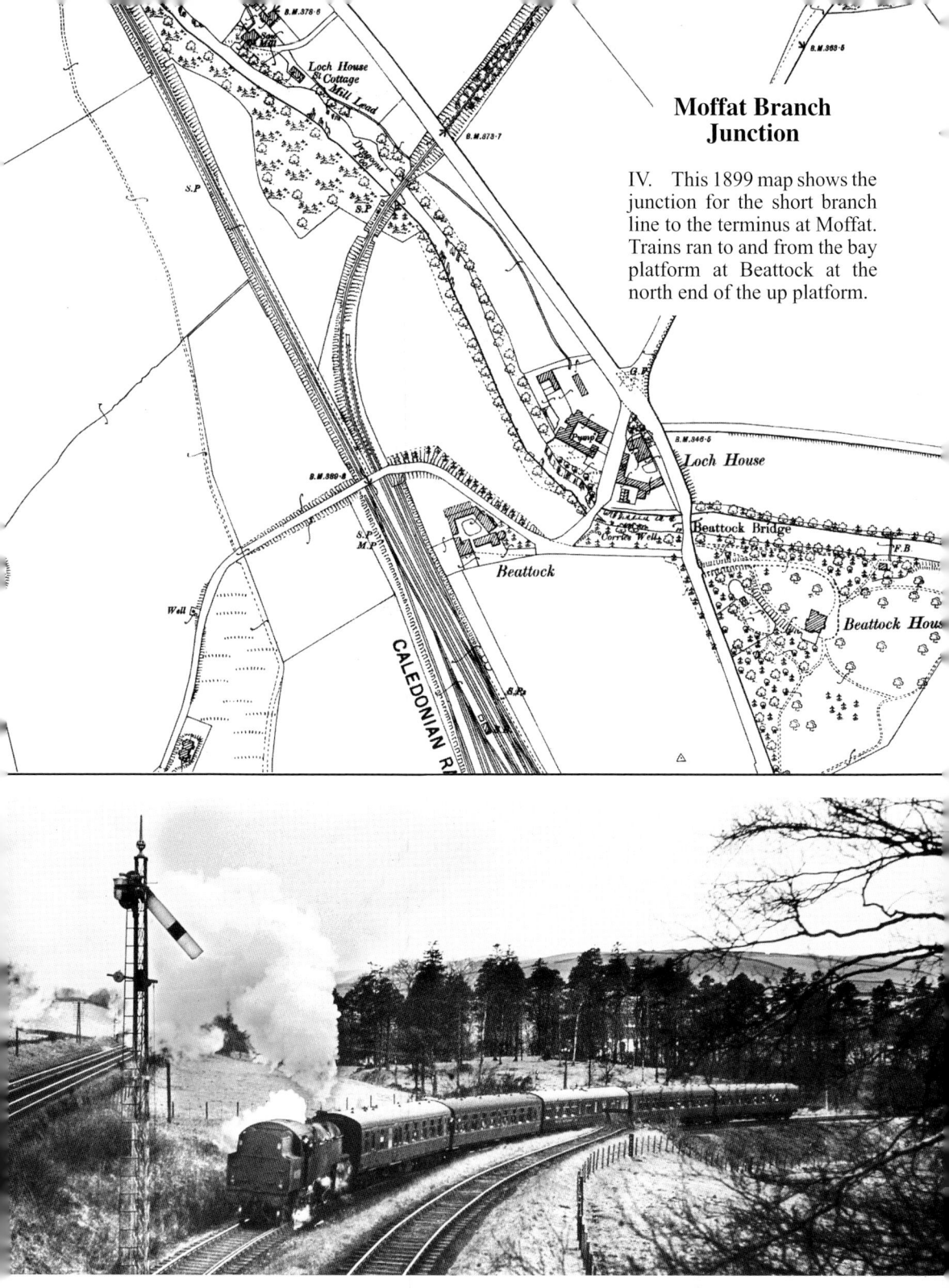

IV. This 1899 map shows the junction for the short branch line to the terminus at Moffat. Trains ran to and from the bay platform at Beattock at the north end of the up platform.

11. BR Standard Class 4MT 2-6-4T no. 80118 approaches Beattock station with a RCTS Railtour leaving the Moffat branch having visited the terminus on 29th March 1964. (G.W.Morrison)

12. A reminder of the sometimes-hostile weather conditions was recorded on 8th January 2016. The truncated remains of the yard head shunt somehow survive for use by engineering trains. (D.A.Lovett)

Auchencastle

➔ V. Seen here in 1899, the year before the short-lived station opened on 3rd January 1900 as a private halt for use of railway staff and their families living close to Longbedholm signal box. The halt closed in 1926 but a one coach staff train ran between Beattock Summit and Beattock station on Saturdays only (SO). The coach was kept in a siding at the Summit and often a banking locomotive would take the train down to Beattock. This train was given a leisurely 30 minutes after leaving Beattock and also served Greskine. The 1952 working timetable only shows a Beattock Summit stop but it is known to pick up and drop off from other lineside locations enroute in addition to Greskine. Passengers could join the train by means of a portable ladder, which was carried on the coach. The nearest town to Beattock with shopping and other amenities was Moffat and this would be the ultimate destination for the train's passengers. It returned later in the day. A new signal box was opened in 1918 and closed in 1939, being renamed Auchencastle at an unknown date. It finally closed on 24th September 1966 when the last working of the Saturday staff train was recorded.

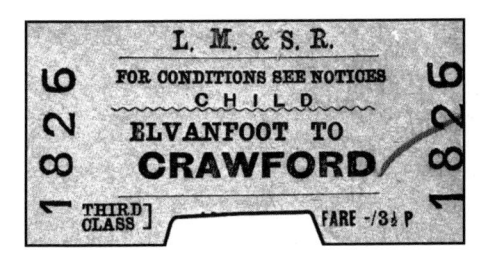

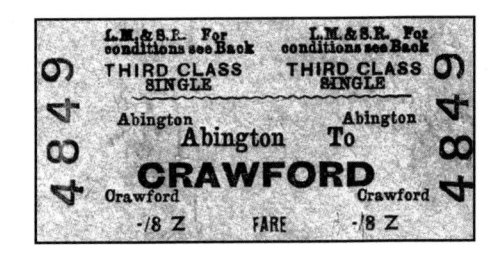

13. BR Standard class 4MT no. 80045 passes the site of the former station with the raised area which was once a platform on the right. The locomotive is on banking duties helping a freight up the hill towards Beattock Summit. (R.Barbour/B.McCartney coll.)

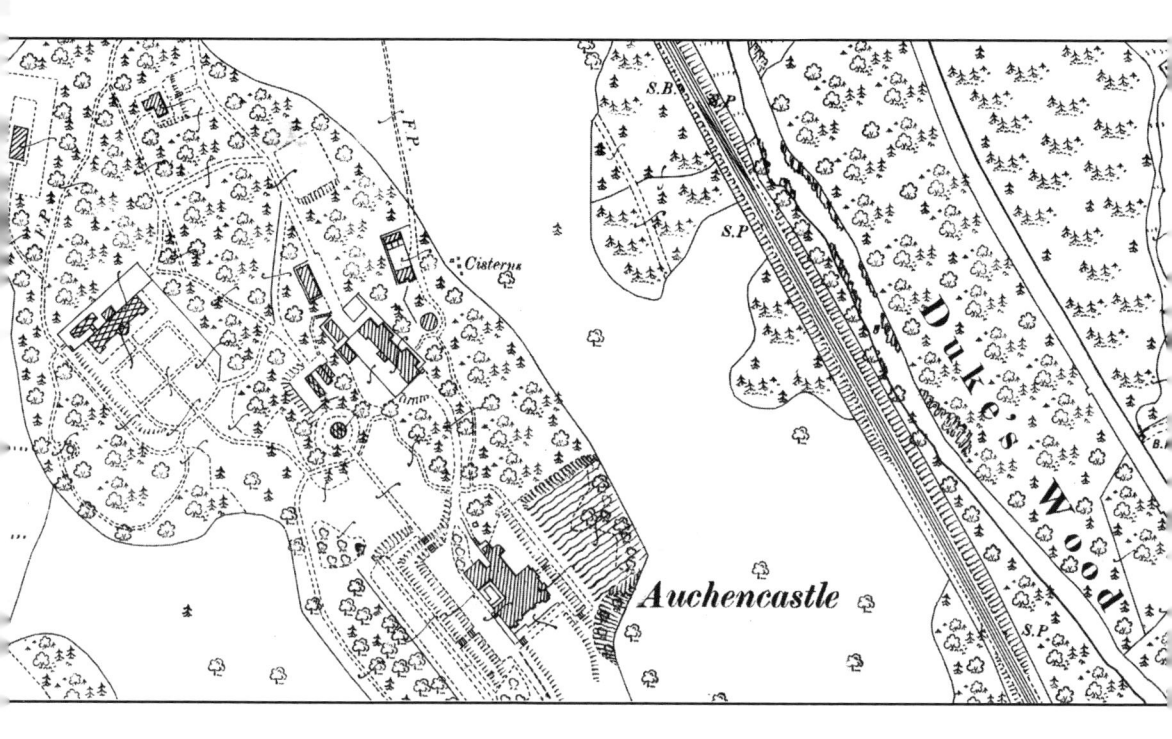

Ruttonside

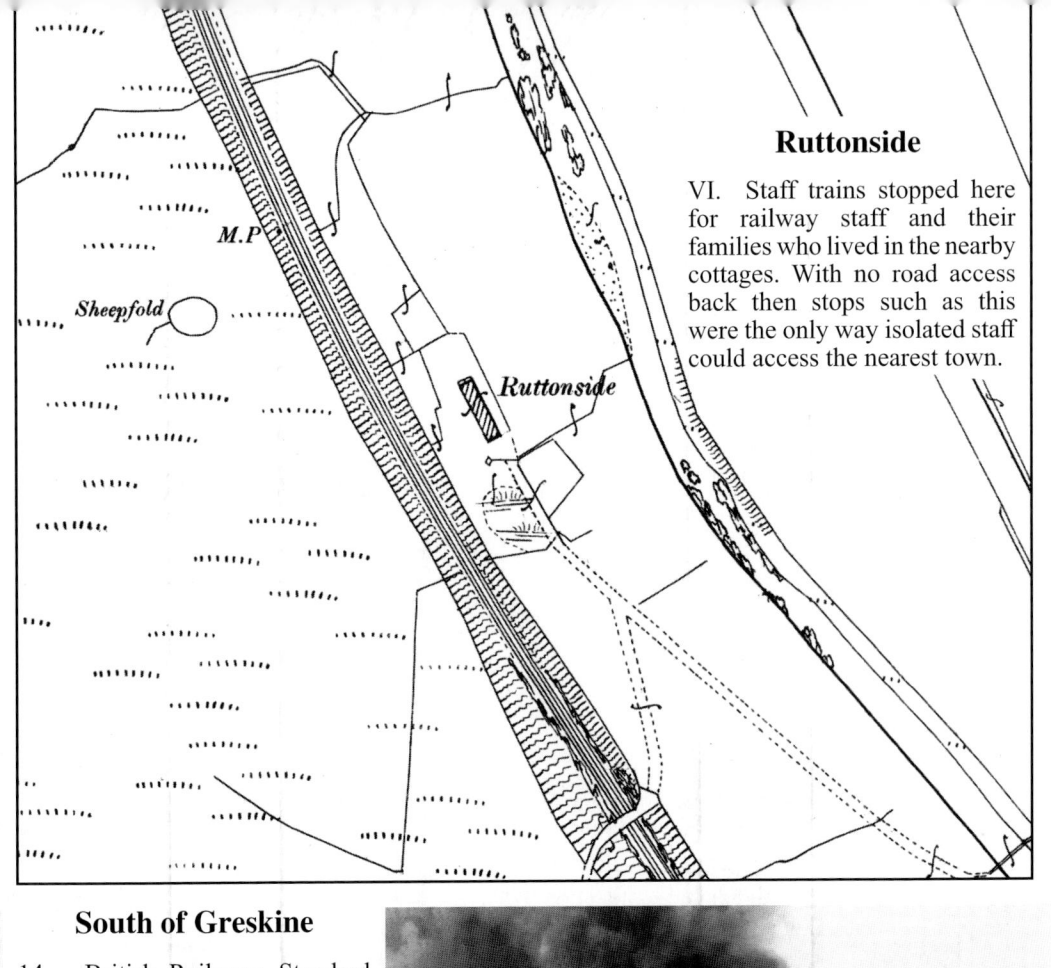

VI. Staff trains stopped here for railway staff and their families who lived in the nearby cottages. With no road access back then stops such as this were the only way isolated staff could access the nearest town.

South of Greskine

14. British Railways Standard class 9F 2-10-0 no. 92012 hauls a northbound freight up Beattock bank near Greskine banked at the rear by a BR Standard 2-6-4T on 12th August 1964. (J.Goss)

Greskine

→ VII. As seen on this 1900 6in map Greskine was another stop for the staff train which served the remote railway cottages. The train is likely to have stopped in the vicinity of the signal box.

15. Fairburn 2-6-4T no. 42192 was on the SO (Saturdays only) staff and family train near Greskine in the early 1960s. (N.Forrest/
Transport Treasury)

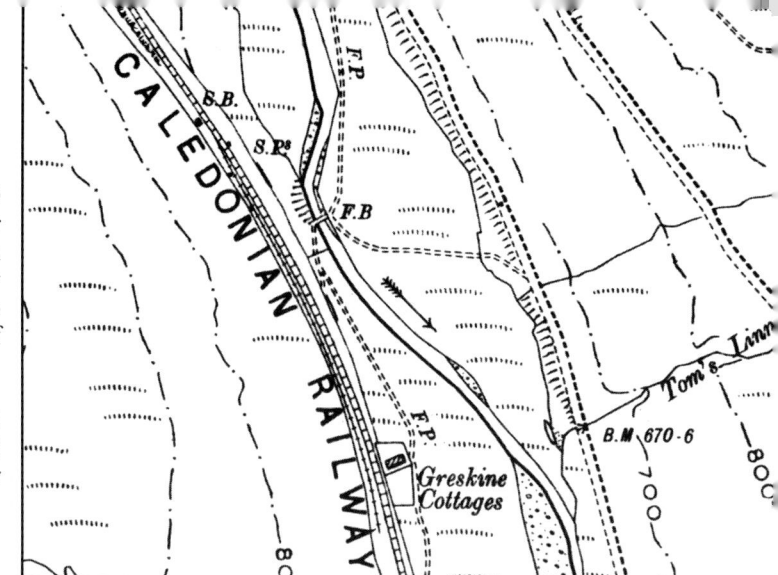

↓ 16. BR Standard 4MT class 2-6-0 no. 76090 passes Greskine box whilst working a Carstairs to Beattock permanent way train on 28th May 1966. (J.M.Boyes/ARPT)

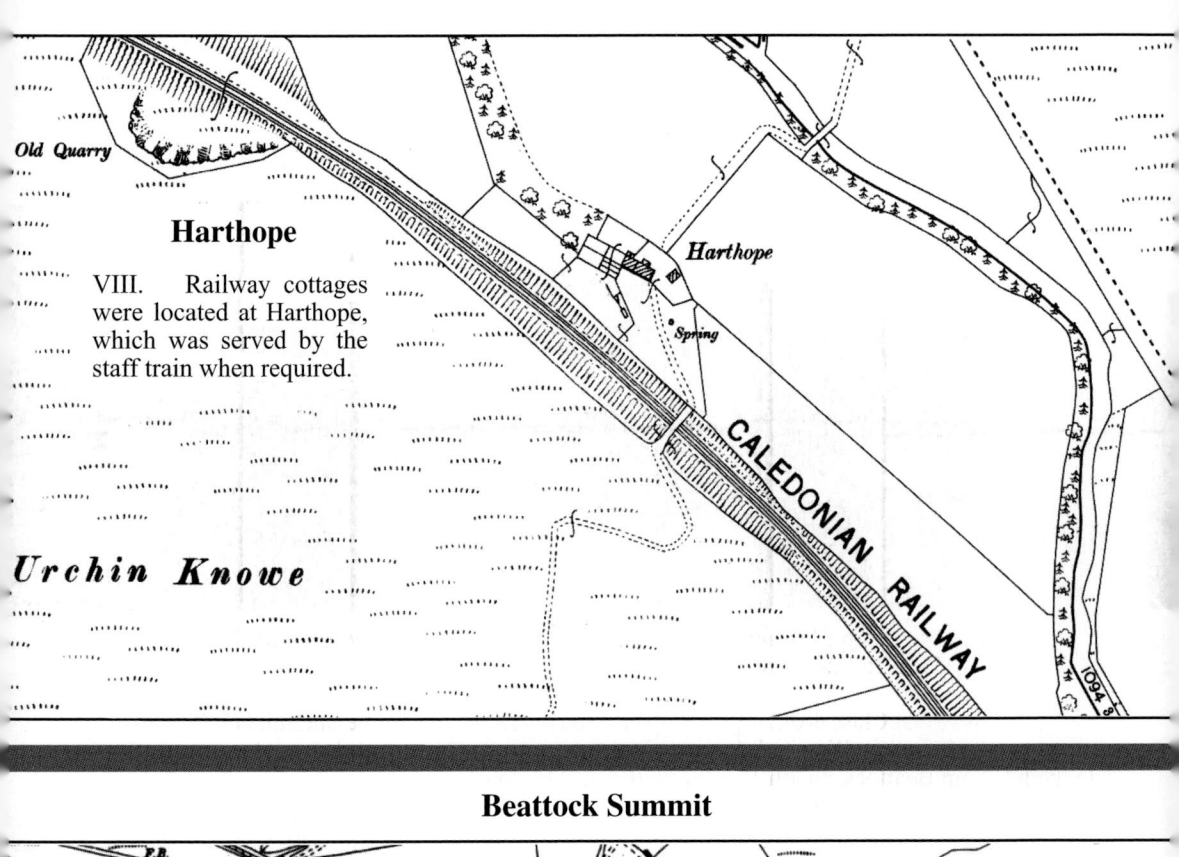

Harthope

VIII. Railway cottages were located at Harthope, which was served by the staff train when required.

Beattock Summit

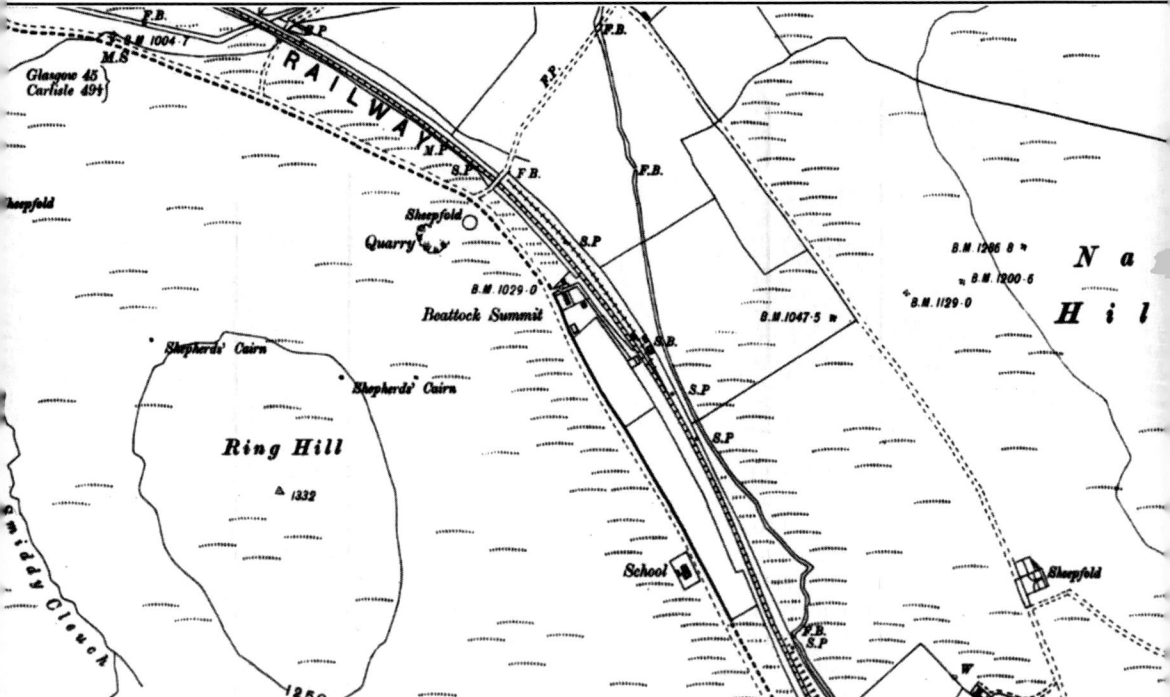

17. Princess Coronation Class no. 46252 *City of Leicester* heads south with the up 'Mid-Day Scot' on 2nd May 1953. (Transport Treasury)

18. Princess Royal Class 4-6-2 no. 46200 *The Princess Royal* passes the Summit box without any exhaust at the head of a Birmingham New Street to Glasgow Central working. It had been banked up the hill from Beattock on 4th June 1960. (G.W.Morrison)

← IX. Beattock Summit loops shown on a 1 mile to 6ins map dated 1913. The summit was 1,016ft above sea level and required the use of banking locomotives to assist heavy trains in each direction. Passing loops were provided here as well as water facilities for banking locomotives.

Summit signal box replaced an earlier structure in 1899 and closed in 1973 when operations were taken over by Motherwell Signalling Centre.

Cottages were provided for railway workers and were served by workers trains usually comprising a locomotive and a single coach latterly working only on Saturdays.

There was a small platform here which was used by railway staff and their families from 3rd January 1900 to take them to and from Moffat, the nearest town. The last staff trains ran on 24th September 1966.

19. No. 42737 a Hughes designed 'Crab' 2-6-0 is seen working the Scottish Rambler no. 3 railtour on 29th March 1964. A coach is standing at the staff platform. The coach was often worked by a banking locomotive returning to Beattock shed. (R.Barbour/B.McCartney coll.)

ELVANFOOT

20. The exterior of the station with the stationmaster and his wife posing for the camera around August 1905. In the background the train for Wanlockhead waits in the bay platform. (J.Alsop coll.)

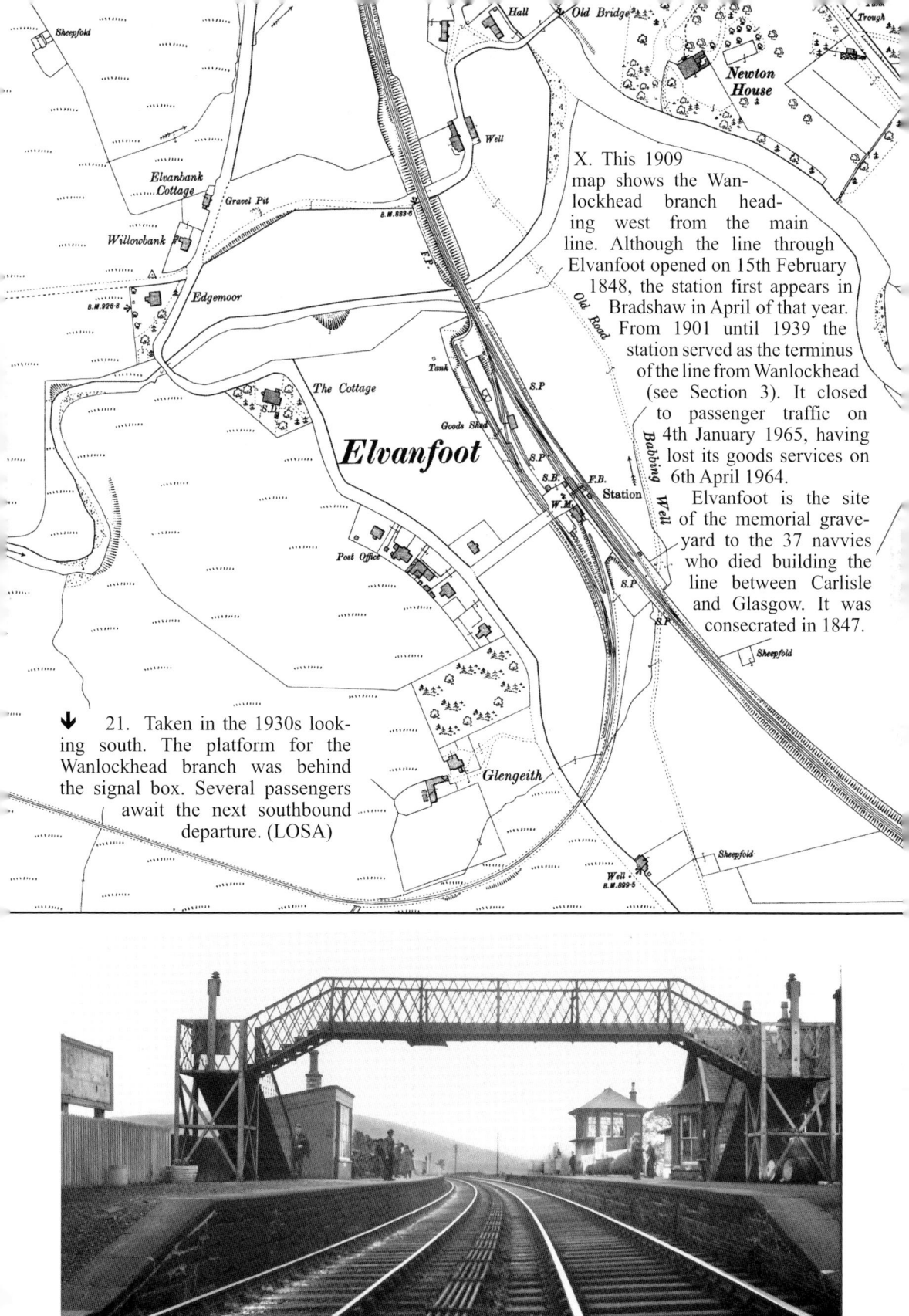

X. This 1909 map shows the Wanlockhead branch heading west from the main line. Although the line through Elvanfoot opened on 15th February 1848, the station first appears in Bradshaw in April of that year. From 1901 until 1939 the station served as the terminus of the line from Wanlockhead (see Section 3). It closed to passenger traffic on 4th January 1965, having lost its goods services on 6th April 1964.

Elvanfoot is the site of the memorial graveyard to the 37 navvies who died building the line between Carlisle and Glasgow. It was consecrated in 1847.

21. Taken in the 1930s looking south. The platform for the Wanlockhead branch was behind the signal box. Several passengers await the next southbound departure. (LOSA)

22. An unidentified Black 5 4-6-0 is shrouded in steam as it passes the signalbox on a northbound goods working in the early 1960s. A section of the former Wanlockhead branch can be seen on the right serving as a headshunt for the goods yard. (N.Forrest/Transport Treasury)

23. Royal Scot class 4-6-0 no. 46115 *Scots Guardsman* approaches the station with a southbound express on 10th August 1964. The goods shed is on the left whilst a single 16T mineral wagon stands in a siding. (ARPT)

CRAWFORD

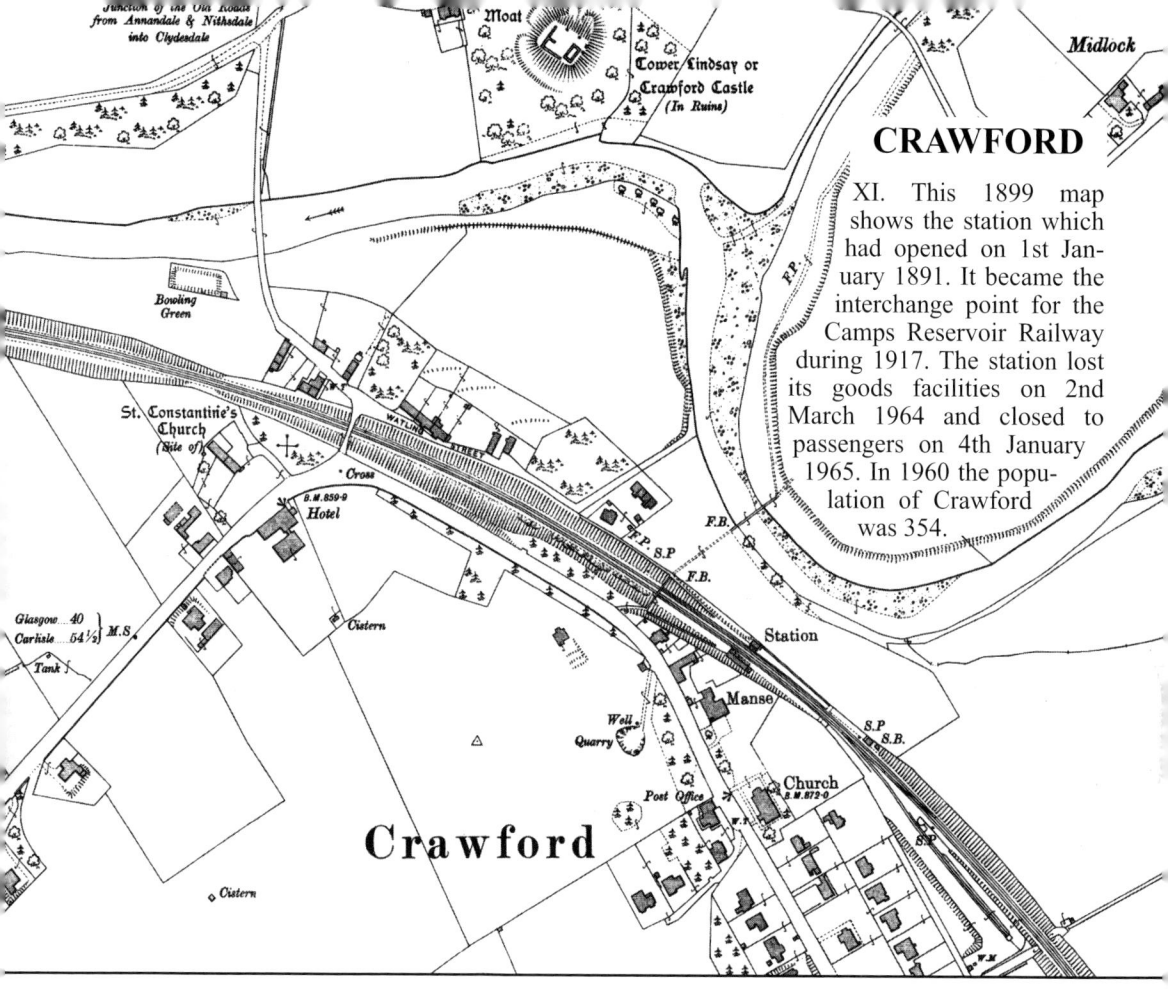

XI. This 1899 map shows the station which had opened on 1st January 1891. It became the interchange point for the Camps Reservoir Railway during 1917. The station lost its goods facilities on 2nd March 1964 and closed to passengers on 4th January 1965. In 1960 the population of Crawford was 354.

24. Looking north in 1904. The flimsy looking footbridge would not pass muster today. (J.Alsop coll.)

25. Looking south towards Beattock, the station nameboard proudly tells those alighting that they are 840ft above sea level. (LOSA)

26. The signal box, seen here in August 1968, was located at the south end of the station opposite the entrance to the goods yard. (N.Forrest/Transport Treasury)

Camps Water Reservoir Railway

In 1917 work began on constructing a 3½ mile 3ft narrow gauge line from Crawford station for Lanarkshire County Council to aid the construction of a reservoir at Camps. It had originally been planned in 1913 but construction was delayed due to the outbreak of World War I. A German Prisoner of War camp was located here in 1916 and some 220 prisoners initially worked on the construction of the railway as well as the reservoir and dam. When the prisoners were repatriated, there was a temporary lull in activity but by 1924 work was again in progress using direct labour employed by Lanarkshire County Council. Additional equipment was purchased to speed up construction. Seven locomotives are known to have worked the line at various times and a village of huts provided at Camps for the now British workforce.

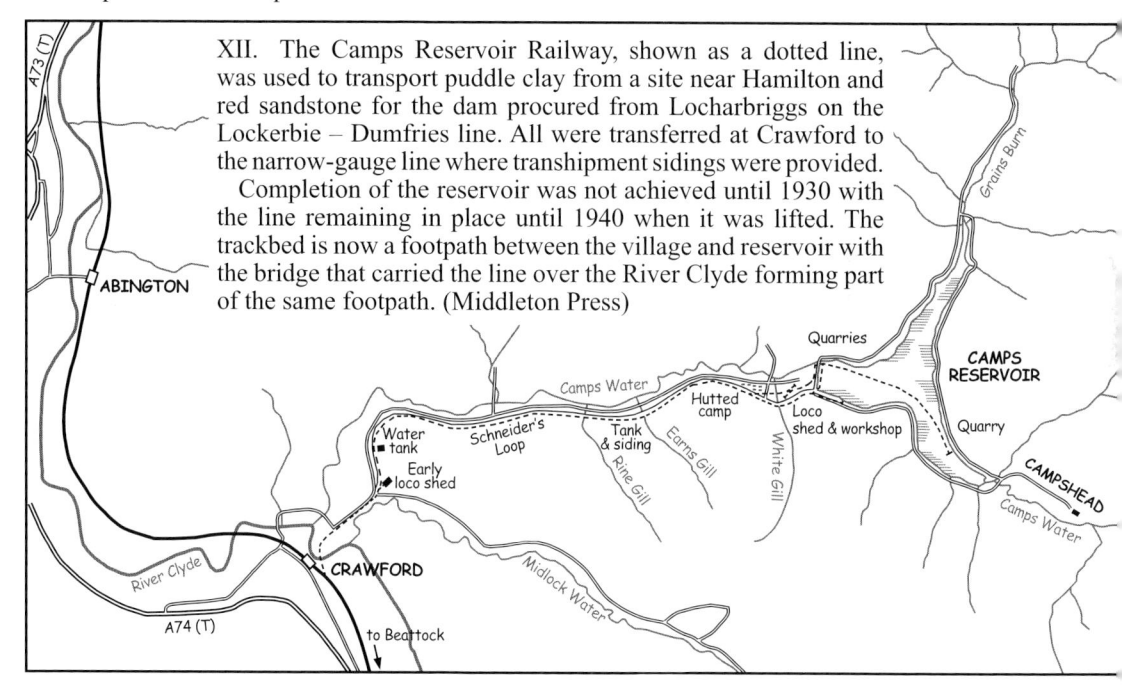

XII. The Camps Reservoir Railway, shown as a dotted line, was used to transport puddle clay from a site near Hamilton and red sandstone for the dam procured from Locharbriggs on the Lockerbie – Dumfries line. All were transferred at Crawford to the narrow-gauge line where transhipment sidings were provided.

Completion of the reservoir was not achieved until 1930 with the line remaining in place until 1940 when it was lifted. The trackbed is now a footpath between the village and reservoir with the bridge that carried the line over the River Clyde forming part of the same footpath. (Middleton Press)

27. This bridge once carried the Camps Reservoir Railway over the River Clyde near Crawford station. It now carries a footpath. (W.Roberton)

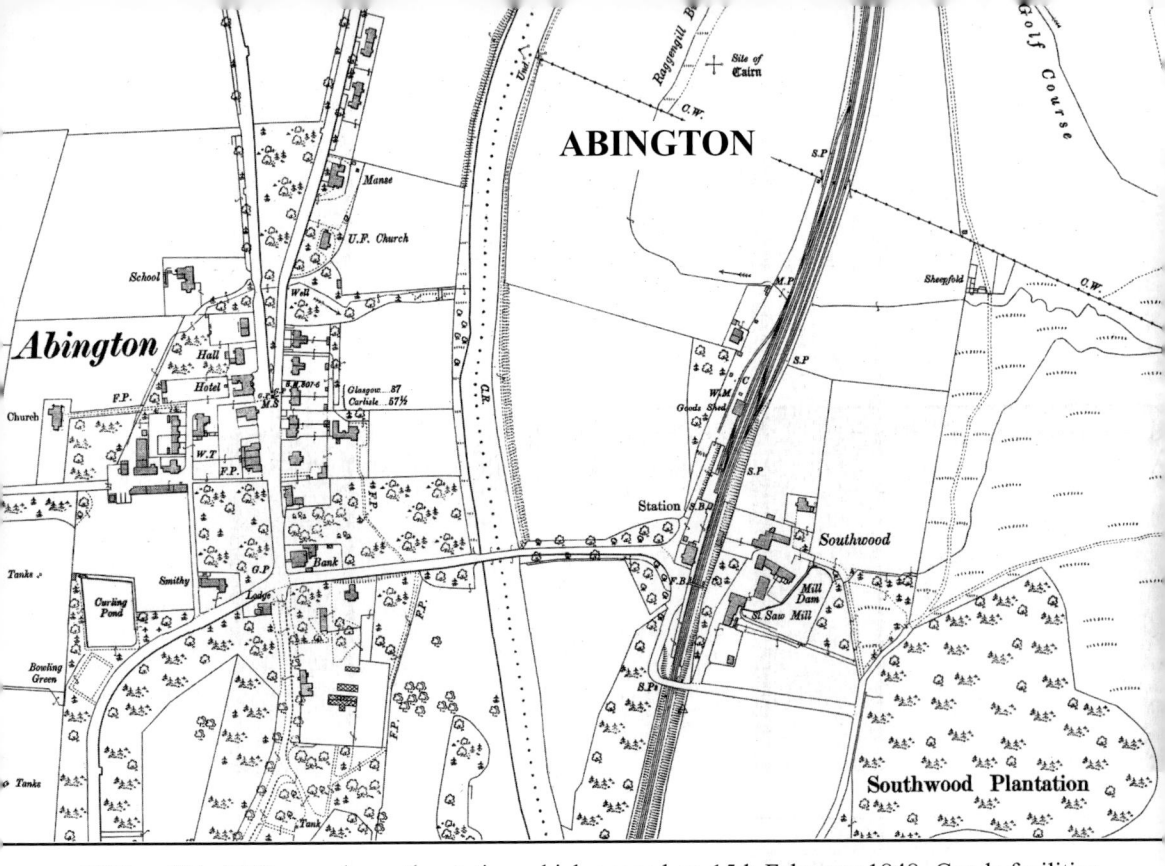

XIII. This 1909 map shows the station which opened on 15th February 1848. Goods facilities were withdrawn on 6th April 1964 with passenger services following on 4th January 1965. In 1960, the local population was just 250.

28. In 1903, the Royal Train pauses at the up platform. During his visit, the Prince of Wales (later King Edward VII) stayed with Lord and Lady Colebrooke at Glengonnar House. (J.Alsop coll.)

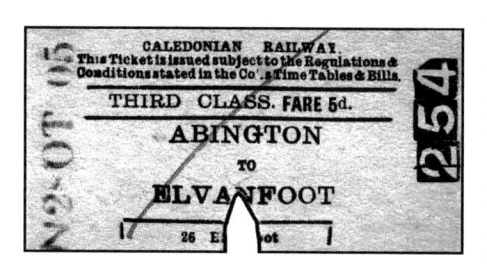

29. The station has been specially decorated for the arrival of King Edward VII in October 1906 for his week long visit. There were plenty of staff on duty pending the arrival of the Royal Train, the King staying, as he did in 1903, at Glengonnar House. (J.Alsop coll.)

30. Looking north around 1930 with the main station building on the down platform. The signal box is on the platform in this view, whilst the station gardens are well kept on the up side. (J.Alsop coll.)

31. We are looking north on 28th August 1960. The signal box has been moved from the platform having been replaced on 20th September 1942 by the new box seen to the north of the station, provided in connection with new up and down loops. These were installed as part of capacity enhancements between Carlisle and Glasgow to handle traffic during World War II.

This box had 30 levers until 5th March 1972 when they were replaced by a temporary panel pending closure of the box which took place on 29th April 1973. Control passed to Motherwell Signalling Centre after that date.
(N.Forrest/Transport Treasury)

ABINGTON.
A telegraph station at Symington, 9 miles.
HOTEL.—Hunter's.
MONEY ORDER OFFICE at Biggar, 18 miles.

We now begin to perceive a distinct stream of the Clyde, which shortly after issuing from its source, from the accession of many tributary burns, becomes at this point, a river of considerable size, and keeps gradually increasing—

"Now sunk in shades, now bright in open day,
Bright Clyde, in simple beauty, wends his way."

This is the junction of the Clyde and Glengowner water. Some gold was found here in the time of James VI.

↑ Extract from *Bradshaws Guide*, 1866.

32. Class 90 no. 90001 *BBC Midlands Today* heads past the Abington loops on 9th February 1994 with a southbound train from Glasgow Central to London Euston during the final days under InterCity management.
(M.Turvey)

LAMINGTON

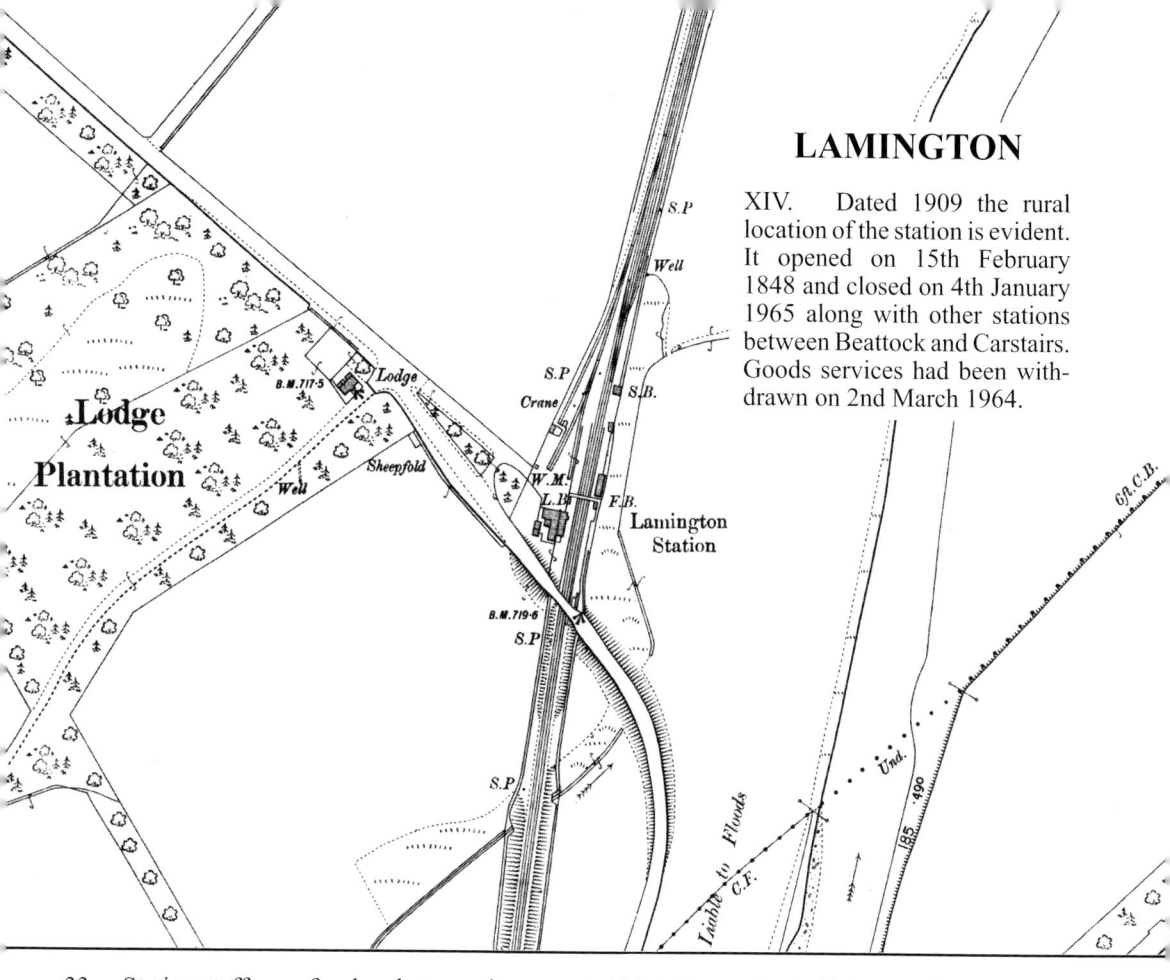

XIV. Dated 1909 the rural location of the station is evident. It opened on 15th February 1848 and closed on 4th January 1965 along with other stations between Beattock and Carstairs. Goods services had been withdrawn on 2nd March 1964.

33. Station staff pose for the photographer around 1912. The station building was located on the down platform. (J.Alsop coll.)

34. The station is viewed looking north in this picture dating from the 1930s. The goods yard crane is visible behind the station building. (LOSA)

35. The station looking north from a period when staff took great pride in the presentation of their station. The neatly mown lawn on the left, the well-tended station gardens and the lack of litter and weeds on the track were very much in evidence in August 1960. (N.Forrest/Transport Treasury)

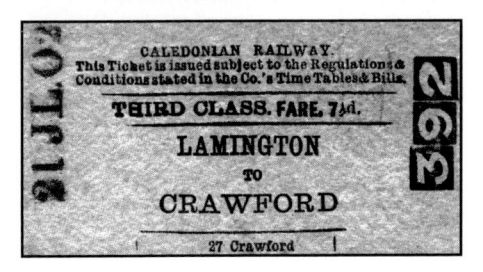

36. Black 5 4-6-0 no. 44921 heads south with an express on 18th March 1961. Built at Crewe in January 1946 it was withdrawn from Perth South shed in February 1965. (N.Stead/Transport Treasury)

SYMINGTON

37. This was the junction for the Peebles branch. Dating from September 1904, this view looking south shows the goods yard in the distance and the island platform building behind which the branch line locomotive is waiting to work the branch train to Peebles. (J.Alsop coll.)

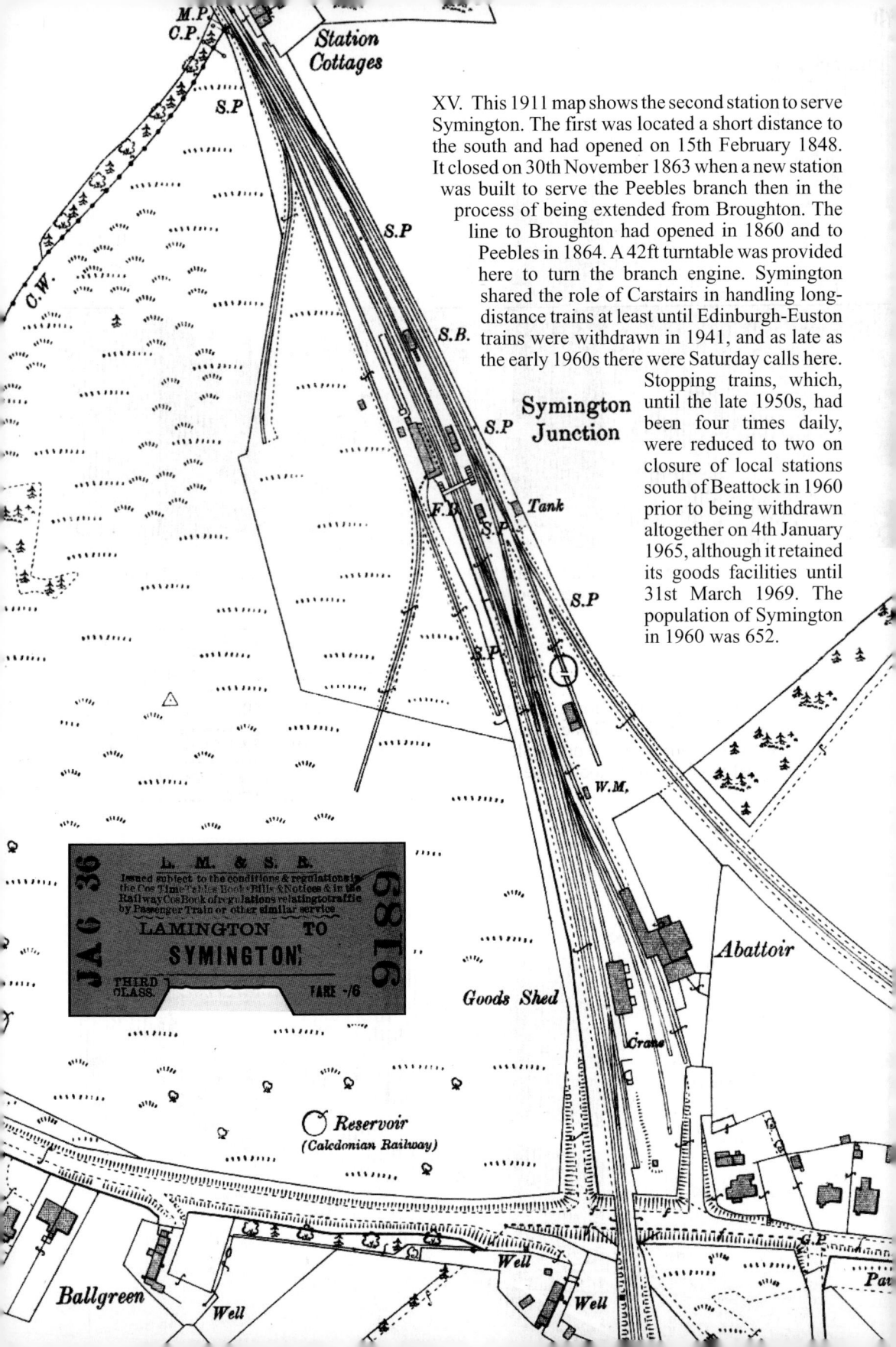

XV. This 1911 map shows the second station to serve Symington. The first was located a short distance to the south and had opened on 15th February 1848. It closed on 30th November 1863 when a new station was built to serve the Peebles branch then in the process of being extended from Broughton. The line to Broughton had opened in 1860 and to Peebles in 1864. A 42ft turntable was provided here to turn the branch engine. Symington shared the role of Carstairs in handling long-distance trains at least until Edinburgh-Euston trains were withdrawn in 1941, and as late as the early 1960s there were Saturday calls here.

Stopping trains, which, until the late 1950s, had been four times daily, were reduced to two on closure of local stations south of Beattock in 1960 prior to being withdrawn altogether on 4th January 1965, although it retained its goods facilities until 31st March 1969. The population of Symington in 1960 was 652.

38. Looking north this picture dates from 1910. Oxo cubes are prominently advertised on the main building whilst the signal box towers above the station. (J.Alsop coll.)

39. The station nameboard proudly states that it is the junction for Peebles. This undated view shows the main building on the down platform and the signal box behind the footbridge. (J.Alsop coll.)

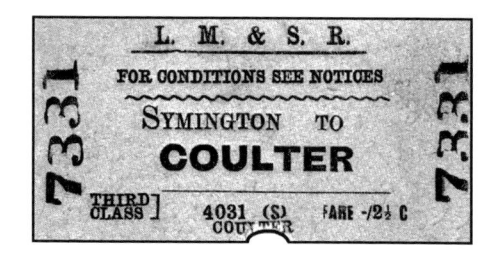

40. A 1930s view from footbridge looking south with the Peebles branch curving off to the left. The goods yard and shed are in the centre with the branch train in a siding. (LOSA)

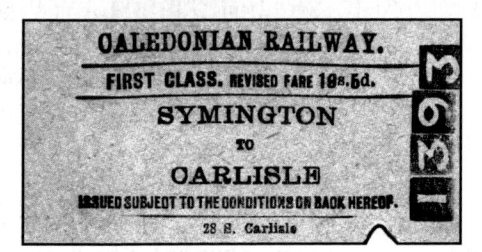

CALEDONIAN RAILWAY.
FIRST CLASS. REVISED FARE 19s.5d.
SYMINGTON
TO
CARLISLE
ISSUED SUBJECT TO THE CONDITIONS ON BACK HEREOF.
28 S. Carlisle

SYMINGTON.
A telegraph station.
A short time previous to reaching the station, we have the famous hill of Tinto appearing in view; towering high above the other giants of nature which surround it. Visitors ascend to the top of Tinto or the "Hill of Fire," in order to enjoy the fine view from its summit.
In the vicinity are *Fatlips Castle*, in ruins, and *Castle Hill*, which is planted all over.

From Bradshaws Guide, 1866.

41. The main building no longer has its canopy seen in earlier pictures although its position can be seen by the marked brickwork. A roof protects passengers purchasing their tickets at the booking office window. This view dates from August 1960. (N.Forrest/Transport Treasury)

42. This August 1960 view shows that the signal box has been moved off the island platform at the north end of the station. (N.Forrest/Transport Treasury)

43. The Scottish Rambler Rail Tour No.3 organised by the Scottish Area of the Stephenson Locomotive Society pauses at Symington having worked the former Peebles line as far as Broughton before working back. Only three coaches were permitted on the branch so two had to be removed at Symington and reinstated back on arrival. Ayr-allocated Hughes Crab 2-6-0 no. 42737 was at the head of the train on 29th March 1964. (G.W.Morrison)

THANKERTON

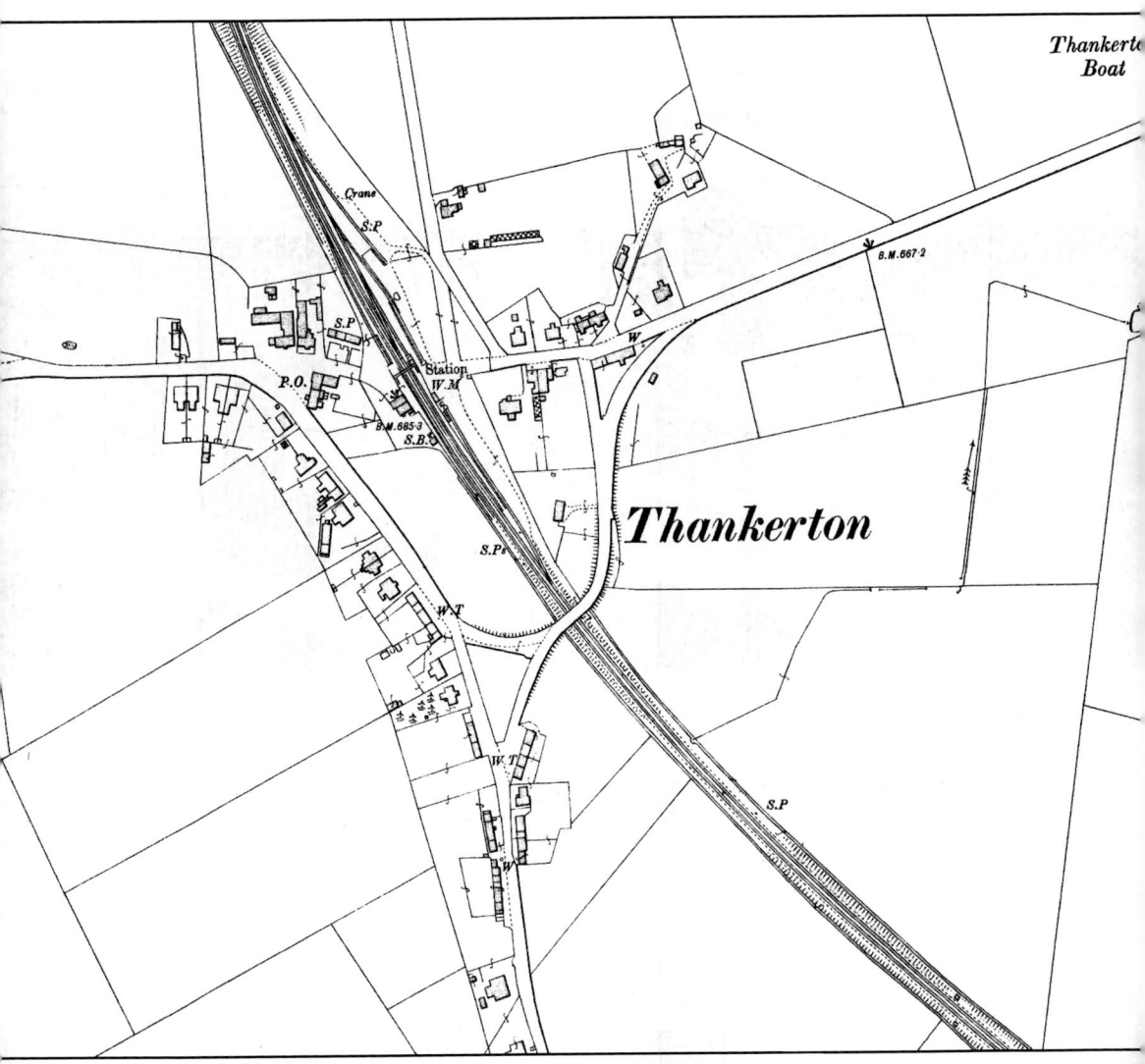

XVI. Opened on 15th February 1848, the station continued to serve the community until 4th January 1965 with goods traffic having finished on 6th April 1964. The map is dated 1909.

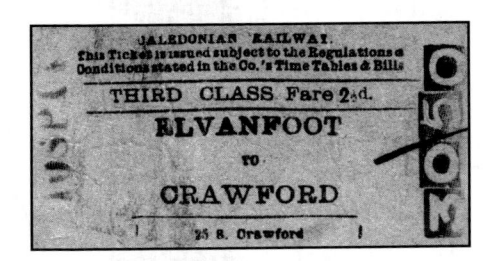

44. This 1912 view shows the approach road, footbridge and main building. As is almost customary, the station staff pose for the photographer. (LOSA).

45. The photographer is looking north in around 1920. There is a fine selection of enamel advertising boards on the down platform. (LOSA)

THANKERTON

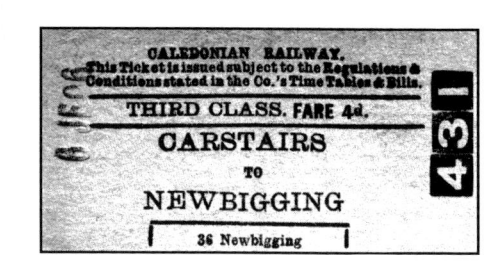

CALEDONIAN RAILWAY.
This Ticket is issued subject to the Regulations &
Conditions stated in the Co.'s Time Tables & Bills.
THIRD CLASS. FARE 4d.
CARSTAIRS
TO
NEWBIGGING
36 Newbigging   431

← 46. A late 1950s photograph sees the station covered in snow. The bushes on the platform are well manicured.
(N.Forrest/Transport Treasury)

↙ 47. A view of the south end of the station with the local coal merchant's lorry collecting from the stack adjacent to the siding. (N.Forrest/Transport Treasury)

↓ 48. Peak Class no. D117 heads south with a local train from Glasgow Central to Carlisle working on 26th September 1964. The station had closed in April of that year and the siding seen in the previous picture has now been lifted.
(W.A.C.Smith/Transport Treasury)

Grange Siding

XVII. The sidings (also known as Pettinain) were authorised by the Caledonian Railway in 1897 to provide a loading point for stone from Cairngryffe Quarry. They were in use between 1898 and 1964, the name Grange being taken from the nearby Grange Farm. The sidings were controlled from Pettinain signal box, which closed on 6th September 1964. This map is dated 1947.

Two sidings and a loading bank were provided here from the opening of Cairngryffe Quarry, which was owned and operated by Lanarkshire County Council. Authorised in 1897, the sidings opened the following year. Stone was removed from Cairngryffe Hill in the parish of Pettinain. The stone was red in colour and used mainly for road construction and railway ballast.

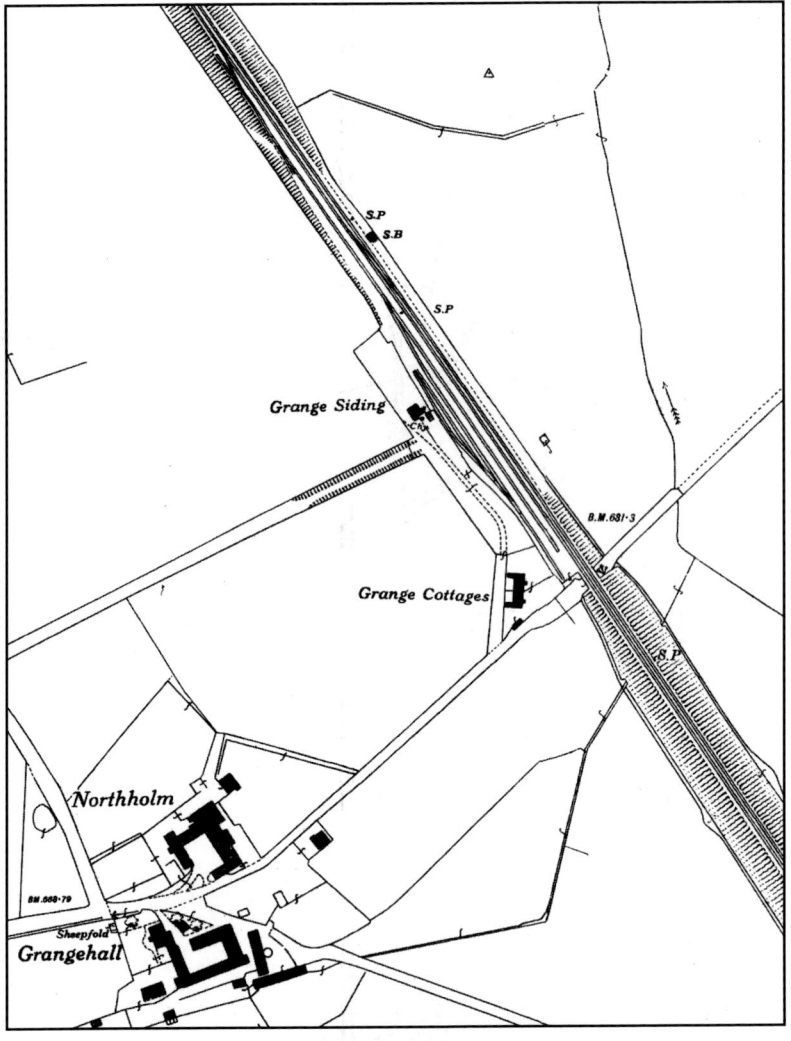

The stone was conveyed from the quarry face to the sidings at Grange 1¾ miles away by a rope hauled wagonway. Trains of eight tubs were worked to and from the loading bank which also contained the crusher. The crushed stone was then loaded into railway wagons for onward transit.

From 1924 a narrow-gauge system was in use within the quarry and a 20hp four-wheel diesel mechanical locomotive was purchased from Robert Hudson, Leeds, carrying works no. 39924 of 1924. It is now preserved at the Statfold Barn Railway in Staffordshire.

The original crusher was replaced in 1926 by a larger one and in 1928 a granulator for the production of chippings was installed. There was however a lack of storage, so all the output was still discharged into railway wagons. The wagonway closed in 1938 and was replaced later by an aerial ropeway.

An adjacent quarry opened in 1982 and was known as Cloburn, which was operated by the Cloburn Quarry Company. Cloburn took over operations of Cairngryffe in 1988 after Lanarkshire County Council ceased its operations there in 1986.

Output from Cloburn was transported by road to the loading bank in the down sidings at Carstairs. In October 2021, Cloburn Quarry Ltd purchased the former Ravenstruther coal loading terminal from former operator Hargreaves. This is located west of Carstairs station on the Glasgow line and will be covered in a future album. Cloburn is a major supplier of ballast to Network Rail.

Float Junction

XVIII. This 6in map dated 1864 marks the former line to Edinburgh as disused. It left the Glasgow line immediately after crossing the River Clyde by means of Float Viaduct. This was the original link to Edinburgh opened in 1848. It fell out of use with trains for Edinburgh reversing in Carstairs Station from around 1860.

The opening of the Dolphinton branch utilised some of the formation and a new direct line between the WCML and the Edinburgh line was opened from Strawfrank Junction in 1872. This was located nearer to Carstairs station.

Only the Lowland Caledonian Sleeper train splits and joins in the platform at Carstairs these days. The front portion working forward to Glasgow and the back portion works over the curve from the station towards Edinburgh following the attachment of a locomotive. The reverse procedure occurs on the late night departure from Edinburgh where it joins the Glasgow portion.

The disused formation is easy to spot on leaving Carstairs for the south and is well preserved today with sheep keeping the grass embankments well-trimmed.

49. Looking south from Carstairs South Junction on 30th April 2021 the former line from Float Junction to Edinburgh can be seen to the left of the current main line in the centre of the picture. (W.Roberton)

Strawfrank Junction (now Carstairs South Junction)

Known as Strawfrank Junction from its opening in 1872 until 1972 when the Glasgow line was being electrified. It was renamed Carstairs South Junction.

A three-storey signal box (high, to see over the bridge) and a permanent way depot were located here. This junction allows direct services from Carlisle to run direct to Edinburgh Waverley, without reversing in the station. The line from Carstairs to Edinburgh was electrified in 1991.

50. Looking south from the bridge at Strawfrank Junction, we see the sidings of the permanent way yard. Several 'Shark' brake vans and ballast hoppers await their next duty. The abandoned line from Float Junction can be seen in the background to the left of the signal. (J.M.Boyes/ARPT)

51. Two class 50s, nos 449 and 423, head south of Carstairs on 23rd May 1970 with 1M20, the southbound 'Royal Scot' which had departed Glasgow Central at 10.00 for London Euston. Cable troughs are standing by the siding to the left of the leading locomotive in preparation for the modernisation and electrification of the line that had been authorised just two months previously. (W.Jamieson)

52. Having been joined in the station in the background, Class 40 no. D210 and Class 50 no. D414 double head the 10.50 from Glasgow Central and the 10.50 from Edinburgh Waverley to Birmingham New Street on 23rd May 1970. The direct Edinburgh line used by today's trains to and from the south heads off to the right. The wall of Strawfrank Junction signal box is on the far left. (W.Jamieson)

Dolphinton Junction

53. Black 5 class 4-6-0 no. 44925 passes Dolphinton Junction box with a train from Lanark to Edinburgh Waverley on 16th April 1966. The village of Carstairs can be seen in the background whilst the direct line to Carstairs South Junction can be seen behind the signal box.

The junction for the Dolphinton branch can be seen on Map XX (overleaf). It is the lower of the lines on the top right. The line above it is the current line to Edinburgh Waverley. Carstairs station is to the left. (W.A.C.Smith/Transport Treasury)

CARSTAIRS

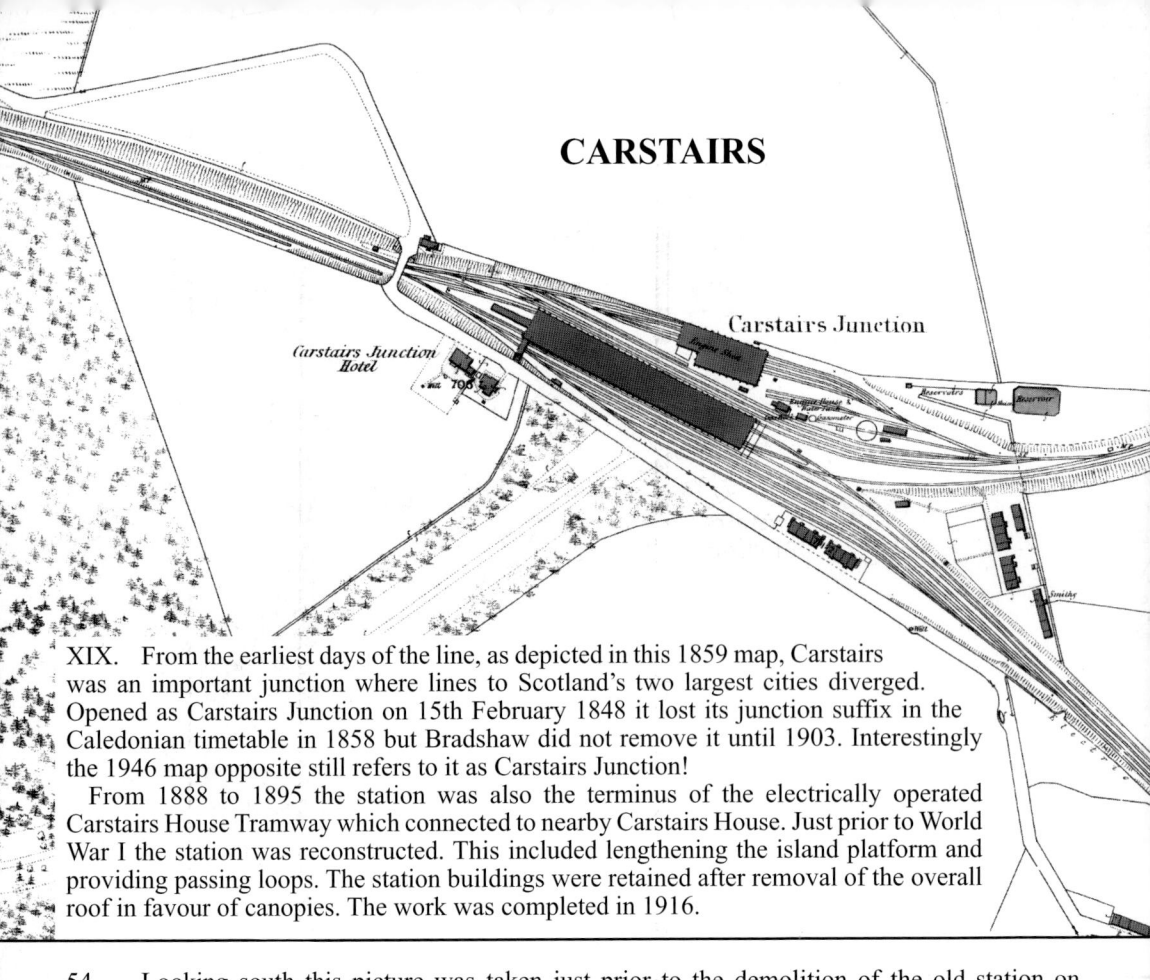

XIX. From the earliest days of the line, as depicted in this 1859 map, Carstairs was an important junction where lines to Scotland's two largest cities diverged. Opened as Carstairs Junction on 15th February 1848 it lost its junction suffix in the Caledonian timetable in 1858 but Bradshaw did not remove it until 1903. Interestingly the 1946 map opposite still refers to it as Carstairs Junction!

From 1888 to 1895 the station was also the terminus of the electrically operated Carstairs House Tramway which connected to nearby Carstairs House. Just prior to World War I the station was reconstructed. This included lengthening the island platform and providing passing loops. The station buildings were retained after removal of the overall roof in favour of canopies. The work was completed in 1916.

54. Looking south this picture was taken just prior to the demolition of the old station on 25th April 1913. The station staff and locomotive with crew have been posed for this historic picture. (J.Alsop coll.)

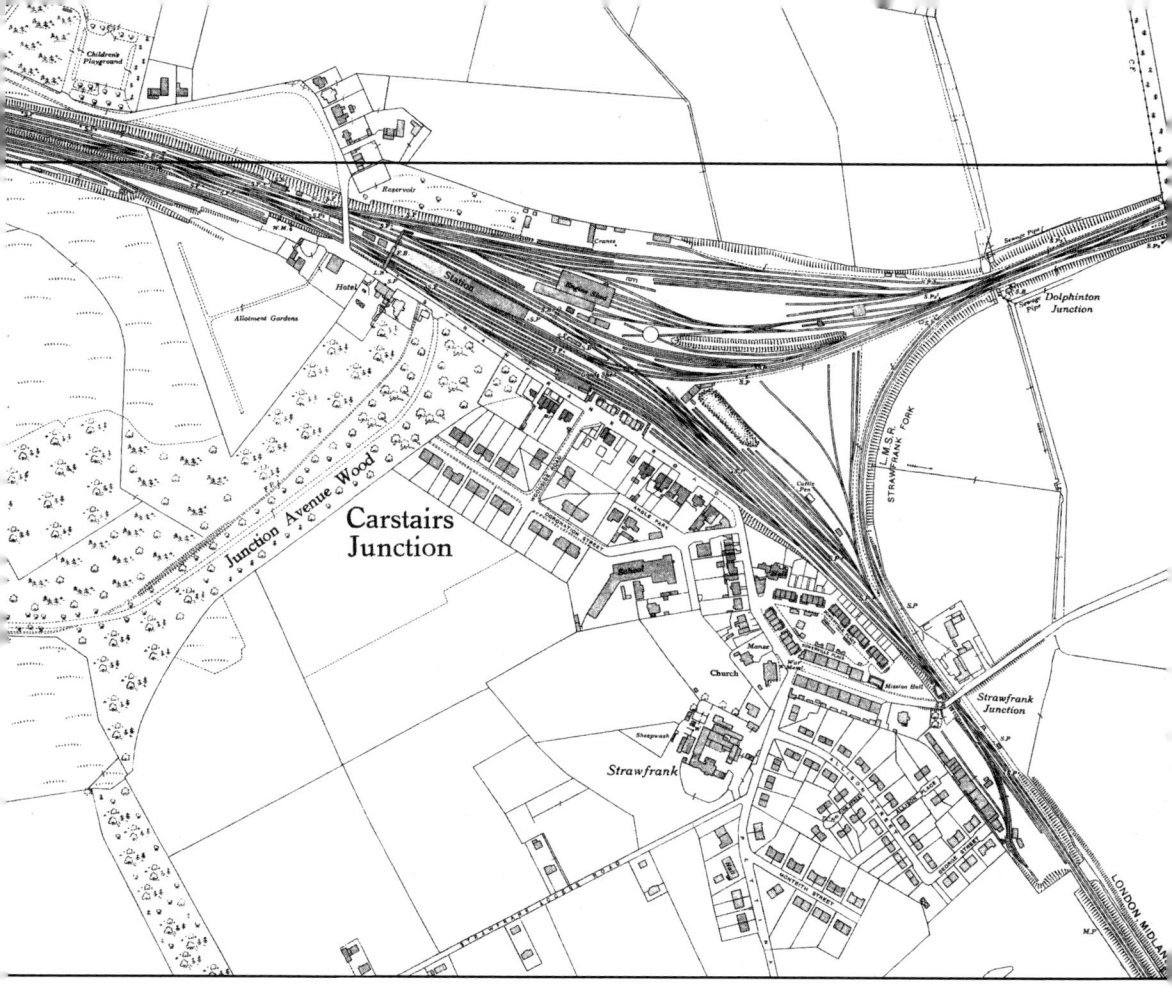

XX. The 1946 map shows the complex network of lines around the station.

The station is served by ScotRail trains running between Edinburgh and Glasgow Central and is one of four electrified routes today that connect Scotland's two largest cities. (Glasgow-Cumbernauld-Falkirk Grahamston trains were extended to and from Edinburgh in 2019, but were discontinued during lockdown and have not been reinstated.) In the past Carstairs was a strategic junction on the network with a major engine shed and goods sidings allowing trains to be remarshalled to serve various destinations.

The old station buildings were demolished in 1913 and replaced with a new structure, which, due to World War I, was not completed until 1916.

The station's most important role today concerns the Caledonian Sleepers Lowland service to Edinburgh and Glasgow which split and join in the station. Since 2001 it has been possible to join or leave the Caledonian Sleeper service here. A daily TransPennine Express service to Glasgow also calls at Carstairs.

Carstairs was rebuilt in 2000 under Railtrack's Station Regeneration Programme and remains staffed. It awaits provision of step-free access. ScotRail has a service every two hours between Edinburgh and Glasgow and vice-versa.

Major improvements to track, signals, power supply and overhead lines commenced in 2021 and were completed in Spring 2023. This work was carried out to provide improved access to and from the former coal terminal at Ravenstruther, which now handles ballast from Cloburn Quarry. The island platform was also improved and the biggest freight loop in Scotland has been installed. It is capable of holding a train 775 metres long.

Goods facilities were withdrawn on 7th September 1964. The population in 1960 was 1,488.

55. Two days later on 27th April 1913, demolition work was well underway whilst the workforce look on. (J.Alsop coll.)

56. A train from Edinburgh hauled by a 4-4-0 enters the new station in the 1930s with the station clock showing 3.10pm. (J.Alsop coll.)

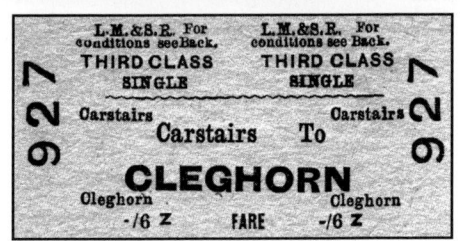

57. Horwich Crab 2-6-0 no. 42741 takes water in front of the impressive signal gantry, with an up train of tank wagons on 17th July 1954. The engine shed is to the far right of the picture. (W.A.C.Smith/Transport Treasury)

58. Prototype diesel locomotive no. 10203 was built at Brighton in 1954. It is seen hauling the down 'Royal Scot' on 13th July 1957 when allocated to Willesden depot in London. It was withdrawn from traffic in 1963 and scrapped in 1968. (W.A.C.Smith/Transport Treasury)

59. LNER V1 Class 2-6-2T no. 67666 arrives with a local train from Edinburgh on 5th September 1959. (A.Swain/Transport Treasury)

60. Heading north past no. 2 signal box, Carlisle Kingmoor-allocated Clan class 4-6-2 no. 72009 *Clan Stewart* has just left the station with a London Euston to Perth express on 12th August 1960. (G.W.Morrison)

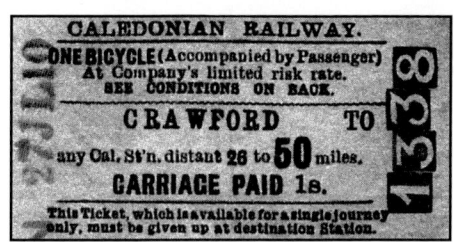

L. M. & S. R.

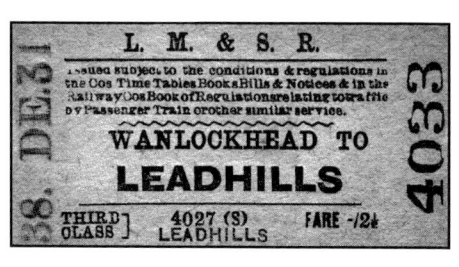

WANLOCKHEAD TO
LEADHILLS

61. Rebuilt Patriot class 4-6-0 no. 45512 *Bunsen* passes on the avoiding line whilst working a special train from Glasgow Central to Blackpool on 13th July 1963. The engine shed is on the right. (W.A.C.Smith/Transport Treasury)

62. Black 5 class 4-6-0 no. 45028 enters the station from the Edinburgh line with a local train for Lanark in July 1965. (R.Barbour/B.McCartney coll.)

63. Stanier Black 5 4-6-0 no. 44802 pauses with an Edinburgh Waverley to Lanark train on 16th April 1966.
(W.A.C.Smith/Transport Treasury)

64. ScotRail class 380 electric multiple unit no. 380107 drops off passengers on 1st August 2012 whilst working a Glasgow Central to Edinburgh service. (D.A.Lovett)

CARSTAIRS JUNCTION.

A telegraph station.

MONEY ORDER OFFICE, Lanark, 5¼ miles.

Here are remains of the Bishops of Glasgow's castle, castle dykes, Roman camp of upwards of five acres, and *Carstairs House*, which is the seat of R. Monteith, Esq.

Extract from *Bradshaws Guide*, 1866.

65. The modern station building was rebuilt in the late 1990s. The single-story building contains the booking office, waiting room and toilets. (D.A.Lovett)

66. An ariel view showing the junction in November 2022. The West Coast Main Line to Glasgow Central runs from bottom left to top left with the Edinburgh line branching to the right. The top of the triangle allows through traffic between Edinburgh and Glasgow and vice-versa. The sidings on the site of the former locomotive depot are to the right of the triangle with the station at the north end. (Network Rail Press Office)

Carstairs Engine Shed

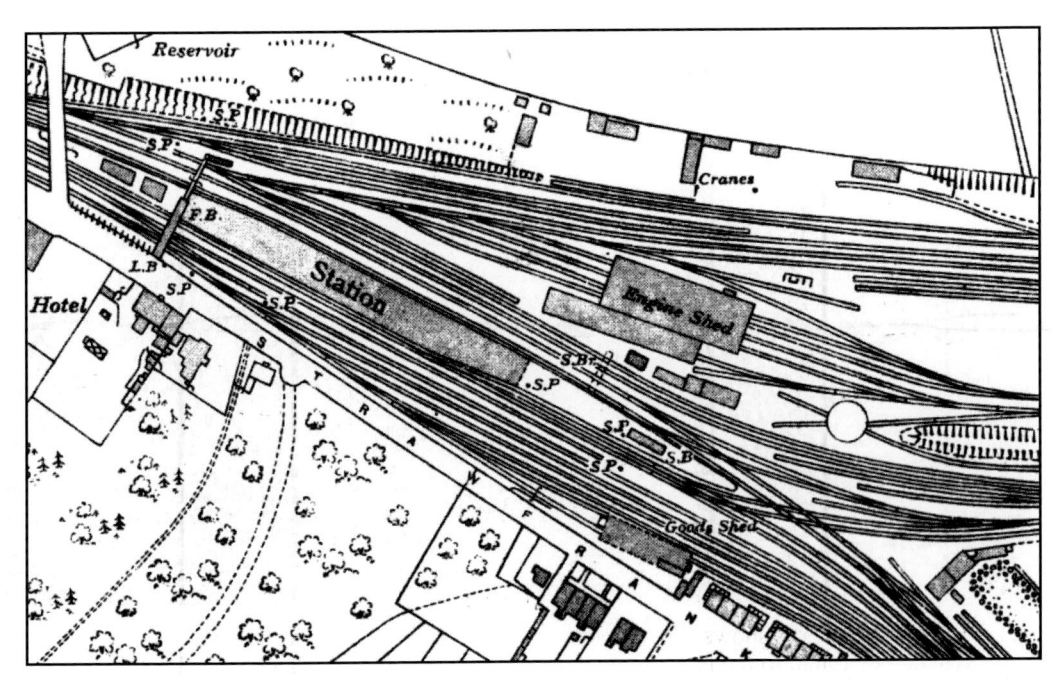

XXI. Carstairs Shed is seen here in 1946. A wooden shed was provided from the opening of the line. It was replaced by a new four road stone shed in 1853. The depot was rebuilt by the LMS in the mid-1930s. The Caledonian Railway gave Carstairs the shed code 27D which it retained from 1884 until 31st December 1939. The LMS reorganised the sheds under its control, which saw the shed become 28C. Following nationalisation, BR too reorganised the shed codes and from 1st January 1949 until 30th April 1960, it was 64D. For its remaining time as a steam shed it became 66E on 1st May 1960, which continued until 20th February 1967.

Having seen the last of the allocated steam locomotives withdrawn on 31st December 1966, it became a diesel stabling point but was not allocated a two-character shed code by British Rail. Following electrification of the Glasgow line in 1974 it closed but was still standing and in use for storage until 1979.

In the late 1980s, the former depot sidings were used for electrification trains in conjunction with the Carstairs to Edinburgh line electrification scheme, which was completed in 1991. Up until this time a traction crew signing-on point remained but came to an end with the electrification of the Edinburgh line. Locomotives out-stationed from Motherwell provided the required diesel traction until closure in 1991. The former shed site is now used as stabling sidings mainly for engineering trains and specialist engineering equipment.

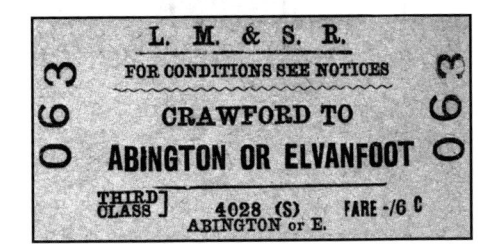

67. This view clearly shows the relationship between the shed and the station. The line to Edinburgh curves round to the left whilst the Carlisle line continues straight ahead. On 16th June 1951, nos 55261, 54438, 57603, 57386, 57635 and 57655 were visible. (R.S.Carpenter)

68. The shed yard is seen here on 31st August 1952 looking towards Edinburgh with no. 54461 on the turntable whilst stored locos nos 54449 and 40903 stand in one of the sidings. (R.S.Carpenter)

69. Pickersgill 3F 0-6-0 no. 57670 on the right leads the line at the north end of the shed on 11th August 1957. The station signal gantry can be seen to the right of the locomotive.
(J.Bell/Transport Treasury)

70. Drummond 2F 0-6-0 no. 57386 is on the turntable on 1st October 1960. The locomotive has been fitted with a stovepipe chimney. The station is behind the water tower.
(W.A.C.Smith/Transport Treasury)

71. Stanier Black 5 4-6-0 no. 45245 stands outside the shed in August 1965. The bay window of the shed foreman's office is on the right. (K.A.Gray/B.McCartney coll.)

72. This 1979 view from the platform shows a mixture of diesel and electric locomotives stabled in the former steam shed or alongside it. (W.Roberton)

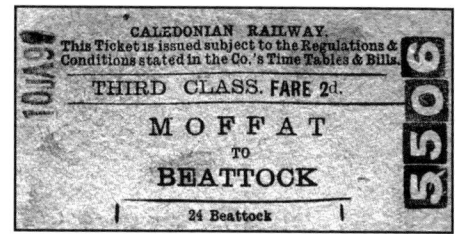

2. Beattock to Moffat
MOFFAT

XXII. Seen here in 1898, the town's station was opened on 2nd April 1883. It closed to passengers on 6th December 1954 and to goods traffic on 6th April 1964. The former station site in Moffat is now home to a Co-op supermarket with some remains of the old platform being visible in the car park. The former toilet building remains as part of the aptly named Station Park with its large boating lake. The population of Moffat in 1961 was 2,057 increasing to 2,582 in 2021.

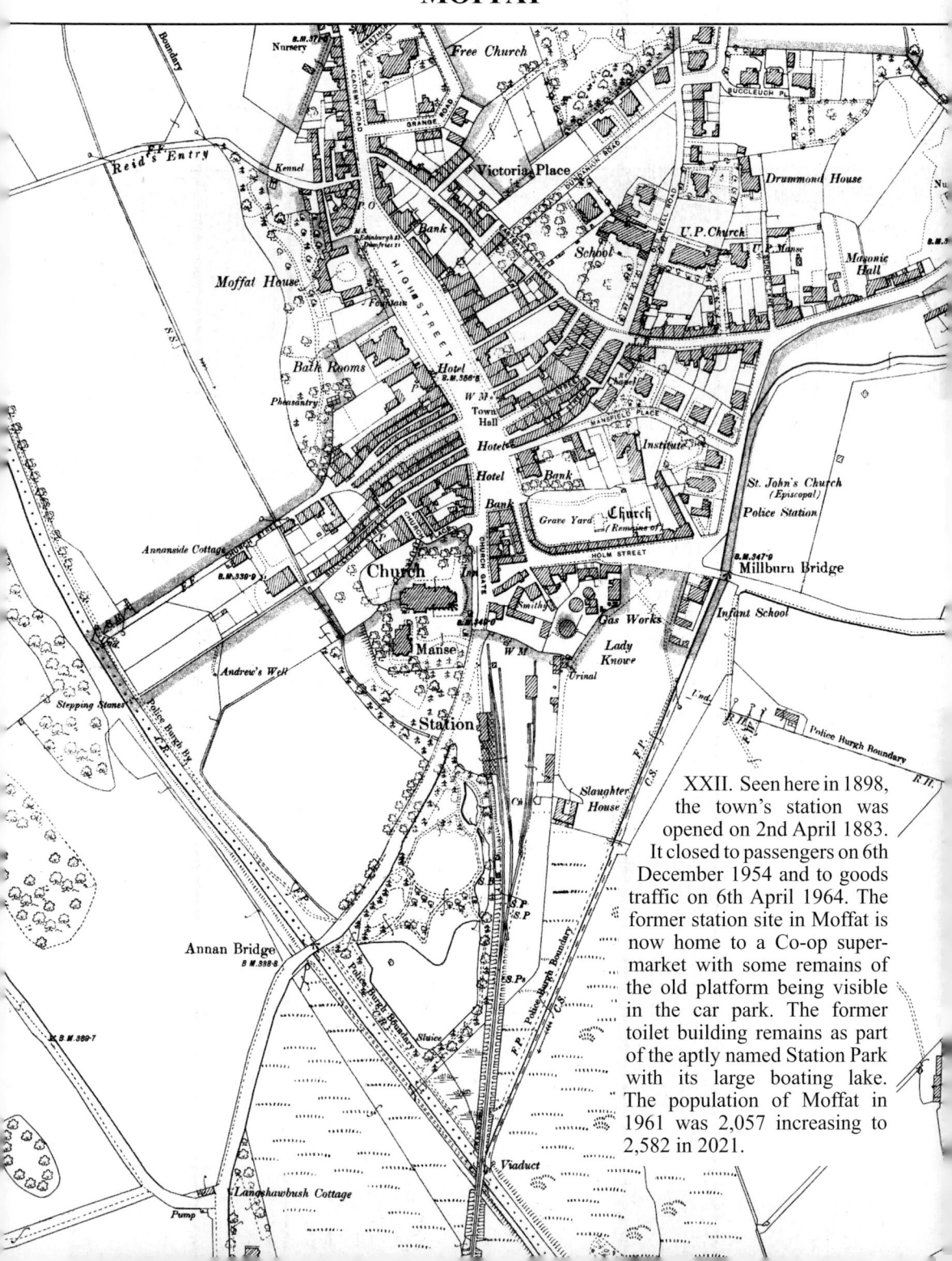

73. The branch line service in August 1931 was being worked by former London & North Western Railway steam rail car no. 10697. (J.Mann/A.E.Young coll.)

→ Extract from *Bradshaws Guide*, 1866.

74. The station frontage seen from the approach road in 1950. The distinctive building on the right, a former toilet building, is the only reminder of the station and serves as a storage shed for the very well-maintained Station Park, which is popular with both locals and visitors during the summer months. (J.Mann/A.E.Young coll.)

BEATTOCK (Moffat).

A telegraph station.

HOTEL.—Beattock.

About two miles from Beattock, surrounded on every side but one by lofty hills, lies the fashionable village of

MOFFAT, celebrated for its mineral waters. The environs are remarkably beautiful, and the different villas exceedingly pretty. Moffat has long been famed for its mineral waters (the sulphur Spa discovered in 1633, and the iron springs at Hartfell, in 1730), and visitors will find every accommodation, including *Assembly Rooms, Baths, &c.* Among the fine scenery scattered round Moffat, are *Bell Craig*, and the *Grey Mare's Tail* waterfall, the latter being one of the grandest sights it is possible to conceive. The water is precipitated over a rock three hundred feet high. In the vicinity are *Raehills*, Earl Hopetoun; *Drumcrieff*, formerly Dr. Currie's seat. The *Mole Hill*, with its camps, and *Bell Craig*, which commands an extensive view, and where delicious whey milk can be procured.

75. On the last day of passenger services, no. 55232 is seen with its one coach train on 4th December 1954. (W.A.C.Smith/Transport Treasury)

76. Decline is setting in during the period of goods only operation. The distinctive tower of St. Andrews Church dominates this view taken in the early 1960s. (N.Forrest/Transport Treasury)

Moffat branch timetable for Summer 1947.

3. Elvanfoot to Wanlockhead

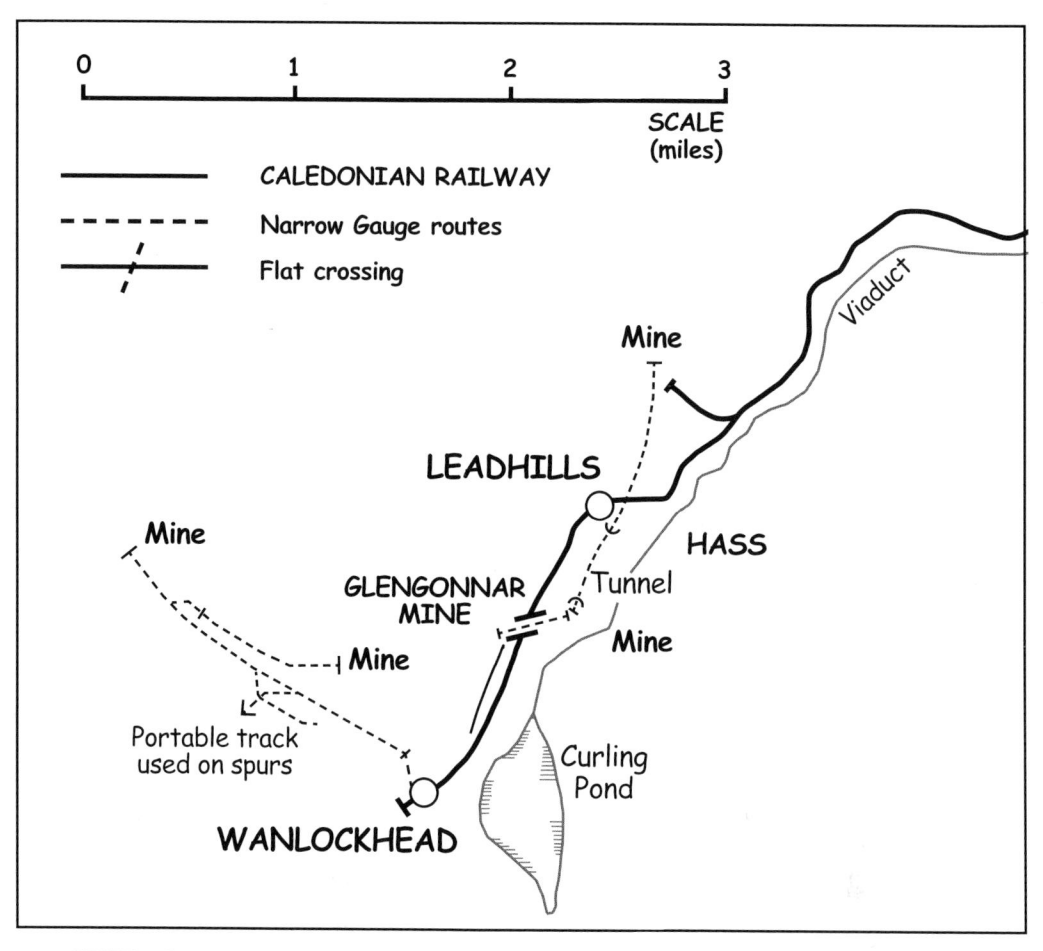

XXIII. Route map of the Leadhills & Wanlockhead Light Railway. (Middleton Press)

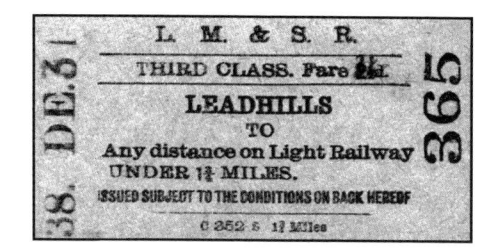

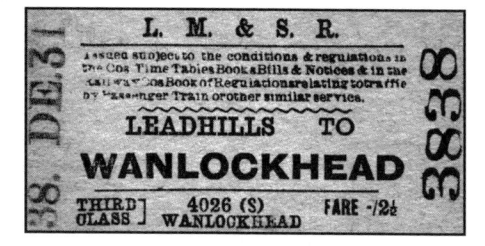

The 1922 timetable for the Wanlockhead branch with four trains a day in each direction.

East of Leadhills

77. The angler seems oblivious to the approaching train as it prepares to cross the viaduct over the Elvan Water. (J.Alsop coll.)

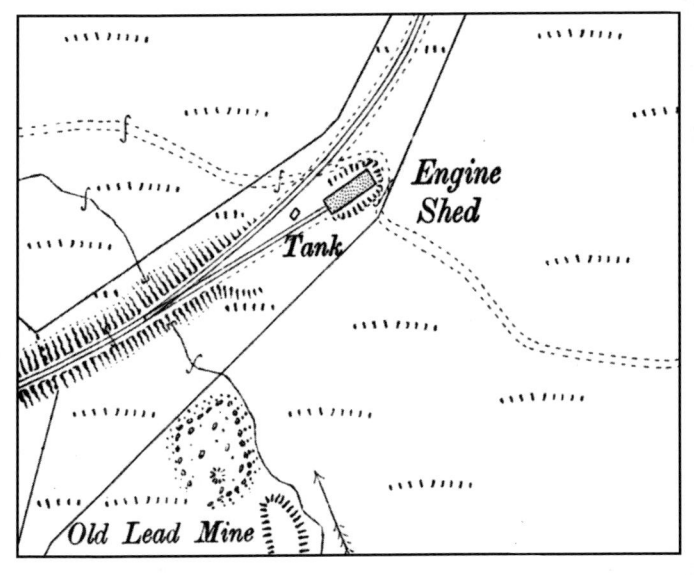

Leadhills Shed (sub-shed of Beattock)

XXIV. The single-track shed was located east of Leadhills station. It opened with the line on 1st October 1901 and closed on 31st December 1938. Its former pit and foundations can still be seen to this day.

78. The shed at Leadhills is seen here on 19th July 1936 with LMS Sentinel steam railcar no. 29910 alongside the water tower. The steam railcar had been introduced on the line in the previous year. (W.A.Camwell/SLS)

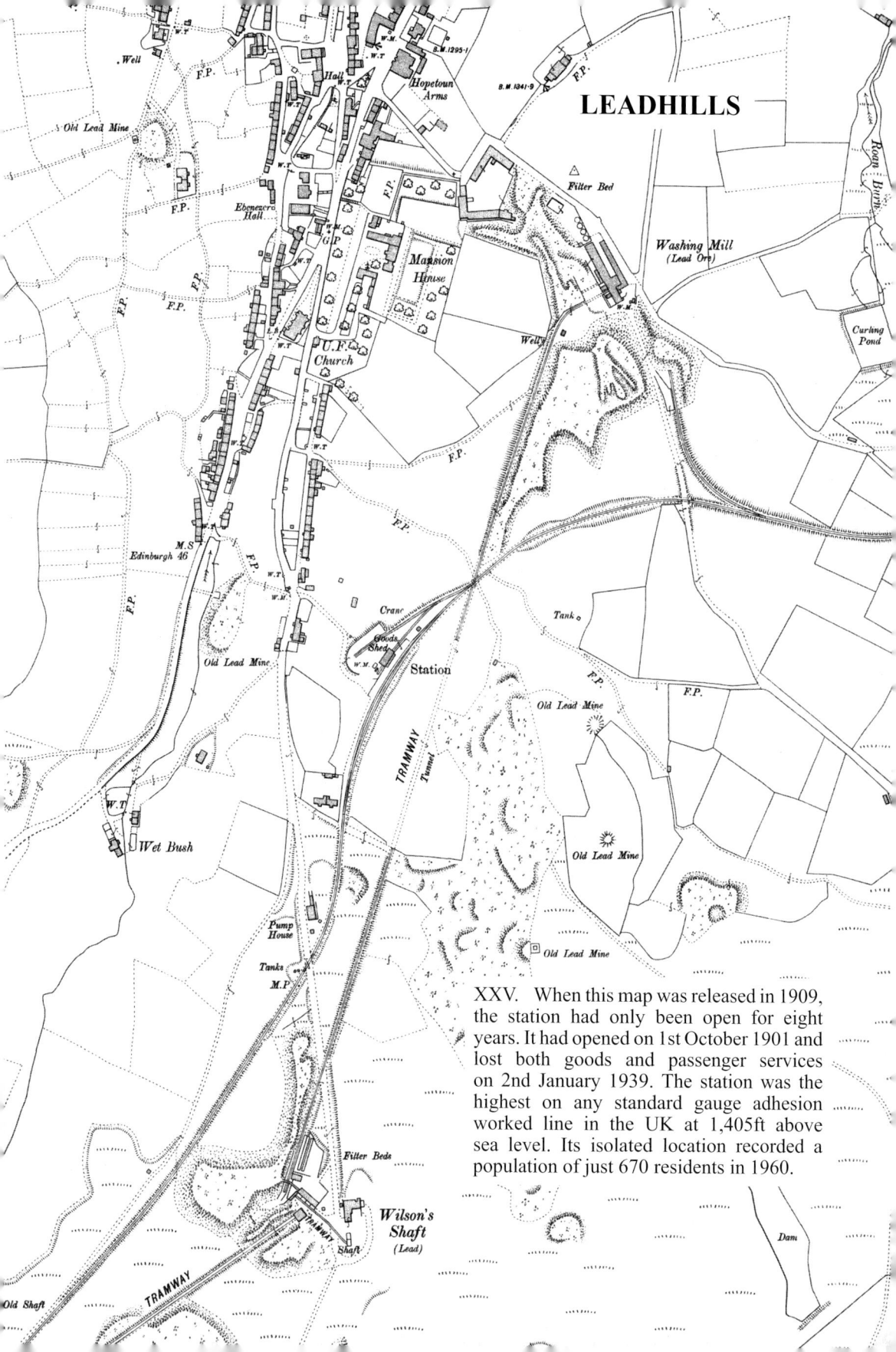

XXV. When this map was released in 1909, the station had only been open for eight years. It had opened on 1st October 1901 and lost both goods and passenger services on 2nd January 1939. The station was the highest on any standard gauge adhesion worked line in the UK at 1,405ft above sea level. Its isolated location recorded a population of just 670 residents in 1960.

79. Seen here in 1904, the station and adjacent house held the distinction of being the highest buildings in Scotland when the line opened as far as here in 1901. A goods train is seen departing towards Wanlockhead. Note the ungated level crossing.
(J.Alsop coll.)

80. Now a narrow-gauge heritage railway, the current Leadhills station is seen here on 6th June 2015. The railway has an impressive array of signals and has constructed a new signal box using facing bricks from the demolished viaduct at Risping Cleugh. The main viaduct structure was concrete, the terracotta facing bricks being added to make it more attractive in order to meet the demands of the Duke of Buccleuch, who owned the land the railway passed through. (G.W.Morrison)

81. A train for Glengonnar awaits departure from Leadhills on 6th June 2015. Locomotive no. 6 *Clyde* was originally built by Hunslet for the National Coal Board in 1975. (G.W.Morrison)

GLENGONNAR HALT

This station on the 2ft gauge Leadhills & Wanlockhead railway opened following extension of the line. Although there was no station here during standard gauge days, miners from the nearby Glengonnar mine alighted near here from works trains.

82. The station at the summit is 1498ft above sea level. The temporary narrow-gauge terminus is seen here on 21st September 2019 narrowly beating the 1,405ft of the former Leadhills station. Locomotive no. 1 *Nith* was built for construction work on the London Underground network. (W.Roberton)

WANLOCKHEAD

83. An unidentified 0-4-4T with the branch line train in around 1912. The wooden station building offers waiting passengers shelter in such a remote and isolated location. (LOSA)

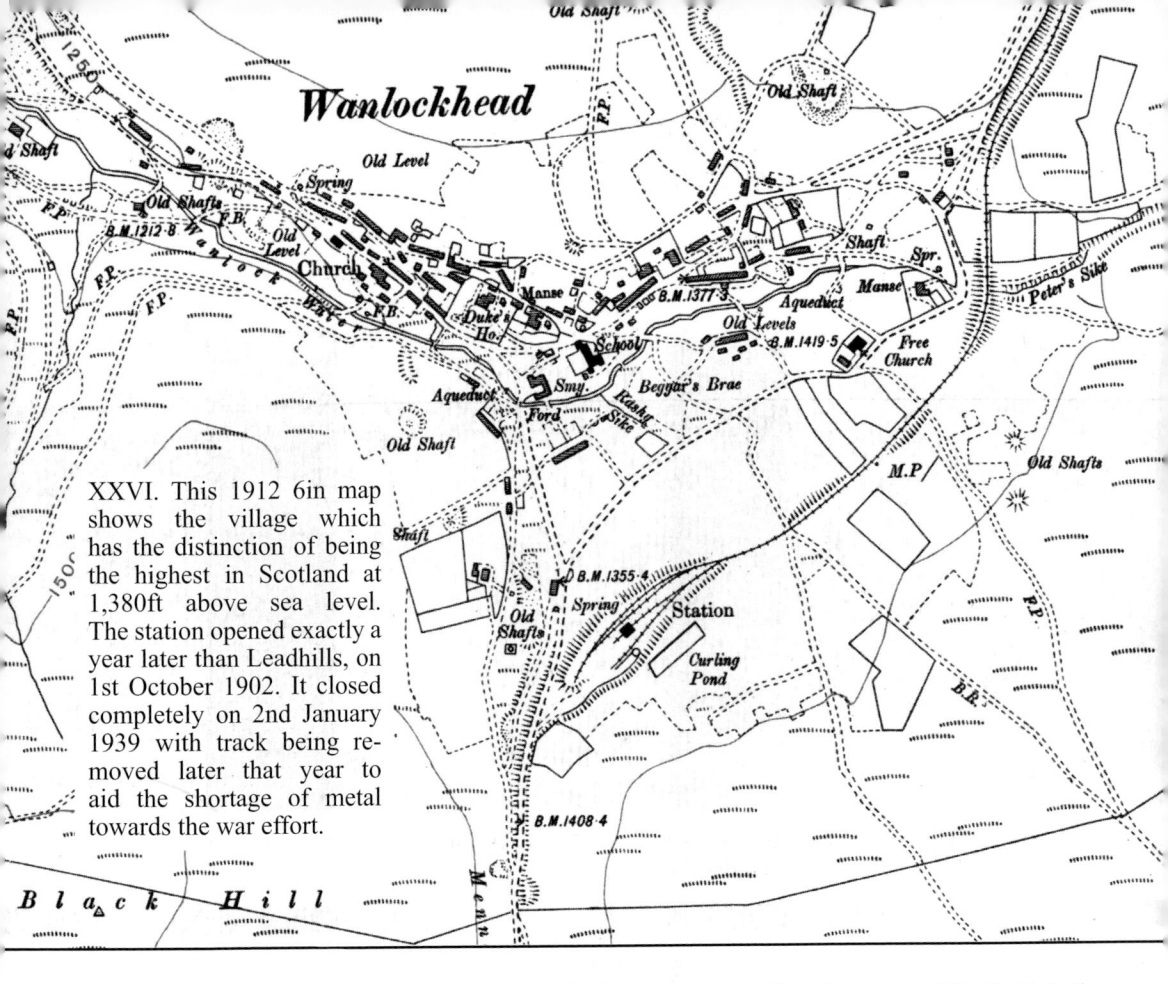

XXVI. This 1912 6in map shows the village which has the distinction of being the highest in Scotland at 1,380ft above sea level. The station opened exactly a year later than Leadhills, on 1st October 1902. It closed completely on 2nd January 1939 with track being removed later that year to aid the shortage of metal towards the war effort.

84. 0-4-4T no. 172 is ready to depart with the branch train to Elvanfoot around 1912. Note the lack of a raised platform and the steps on the coach sides to allow passengers to get on and off the coaches. (LOSA)

4. Symington to Peebles (CR)
WEST OF COULTER

85. The same train as seen in pictures 19 and 43 is seen crossing the River Clyde on the approach to Coulter station on 29th March 1964. (W.A.C.Smith/Transport Treasury)

COULTER

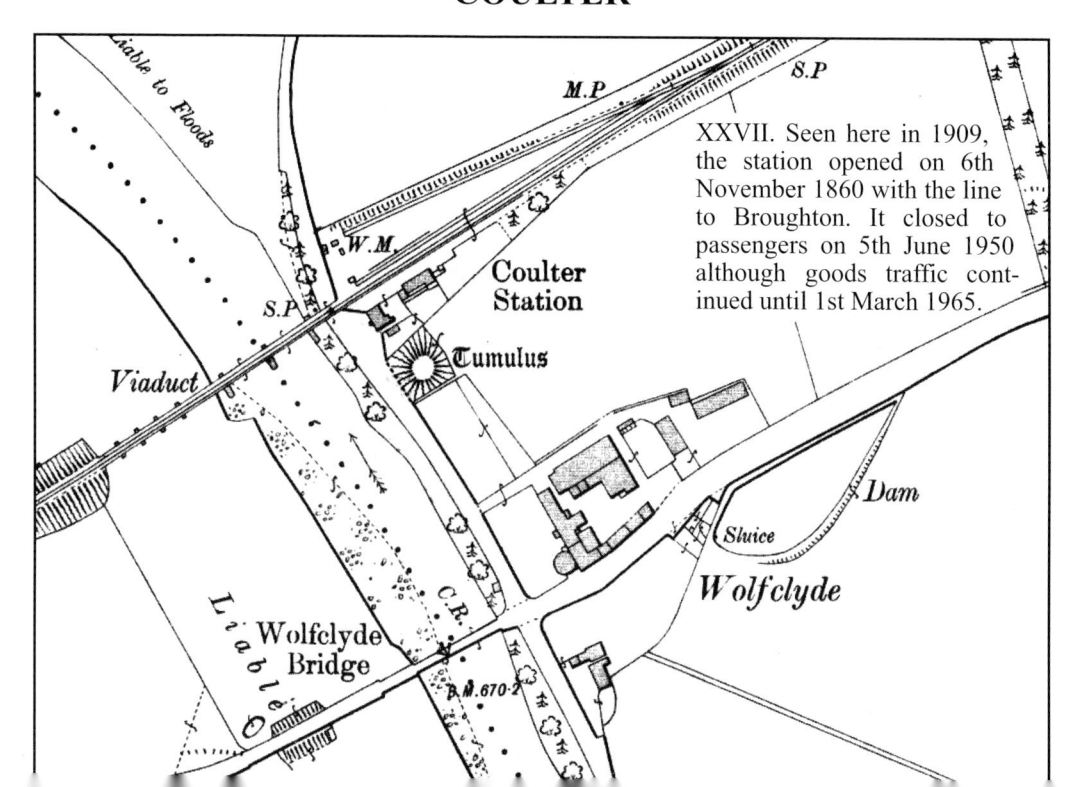

XXVII. Seen here in 1909, the station opened on 6th November 1860 with the line to Broughton. It closed to passengers on 5th June 1950 although goods traffic continued until 1st March 1965.

86. The station gardens remain well-kept despite the station only catering for goods traffic when visited on 1st June 1953. (C.J.B.Sanderson/ARPT)

87. Looking east towards Broughton five years after the station lost its passenger services. Seen here on 22nd August 1955, the goods siding is host to a three-plank wagon with a loaded container. (W.A.C.Smith/Transport Treasury)

88. The level crossing and station building are seen here in August 1960 although the siding is now only just visible through the weeds.
(N.Forrest/
Transport Treasury)

Cowgill Reservoir Railway

XXVIII. In 1892, the Airdire & Coatbridge Water Company was granted an Act of Parliament to construct a reservoir above Coulter. This was the first of four reservoirs to be built in the area covered by this album.

John Best of Edinburgh was the contractor for the upper reservoir, and he would also be involved with the building of the Talla reservoir. With the need to transport large amounts of puddle clay to stop water leakage, it was initially hauled by traction engines. Difficulties arose in winter on the minor roads from Coulter station, on the Symington to Peebles line, with the traction engines being unable to work in bad weather or due to frequent breakdowns.

A 3ft gauge railway was, therefore, built from a black hut near the parish boundary which separated Coulter from Lamington. It was some two miles long and locomotive worked but we have no record of which of Best's locomotives were employed on the scheme.

Construction work on the reservoir was completed in 1899 when it began filling. Work on a second reservoir (Lower) began under a different Act dated 1899 and using a different contractor, David Waddell. Work began in the Summer of 1900 and was completed by 1903. A narrow-gauge line was used for the conveyance of puddle clay within the Lower reservoir itself, which is likely to have been brought in by traction engines one of which was involved in a fatality in 1901 when it toppled over a bridge and into a stream. The Upper and Lower reservoirs are a mile apart. (Middleton Press)

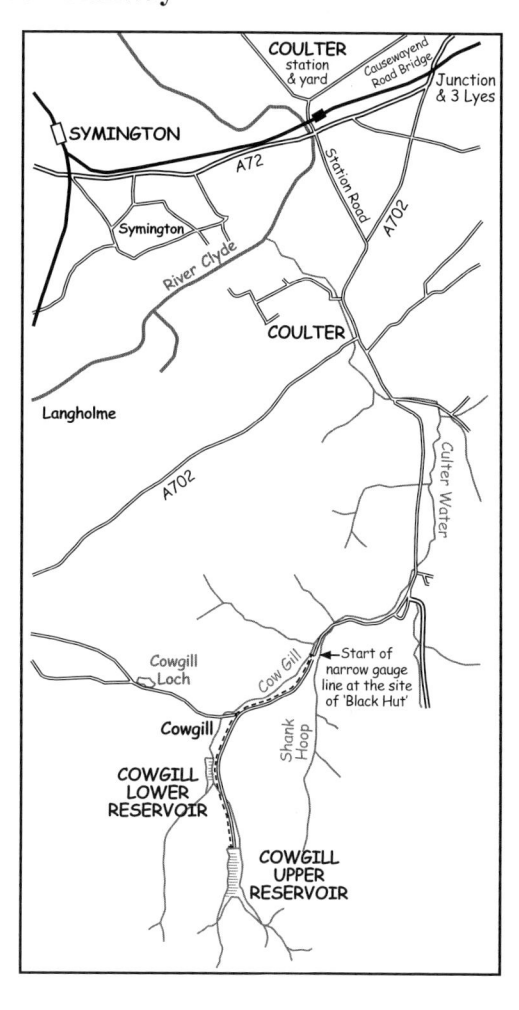

Culter Waterhead Railway

XXIX. The next valley to the east of Cowgill saw a further reservoir authorised in 1900 to supply water to Motherwell and Wishaw.

A temporary standard gauge line ran from the junction and three interchange sidings at Causewayend which was located south west of Biggar on the Coulter Road (A702). It was used to transport materials for the construction of the reservoir authorised in 1900. The line was constructed by Robert McAlpine & Son and was available for traffic from 1903 and was some 7½ miles in length following the course of the Culter Water. A 3ft narrow gauge system was used on the bed of the reservoir using portable track that could be moved to where it was needed, the system using steam locomotives.

The line ran alongside the A702 road for 2½ miles to reach Coulter village where the line left the road to take its own route to reach the construction site. Here a temporary village was constructed for the workers along with a grocery shop, mission hall and school. An engine shed was built and there were extensive sidings to receive the puddle clay.

Three standard gauge and three narrow gauge locomotives are known to have worked on the project.

The narrow-gauge system was out of use by 1907 and the standard gauge line was then dismantled. The reservoir is fed by several water courses including the Culter Water. The reservoir began to fill in 1908, reaching capacity of 500 million gallons the following year. (A.E.Young)

89. The temporary village created for the workforce working on the construction of the reservoir. Trains can be seen in operation in the distance above the buildings whilst the wagons in the foreground have some interesting loads in addition to the puddle clay. (J.Alsop coll.)

BIGGAR

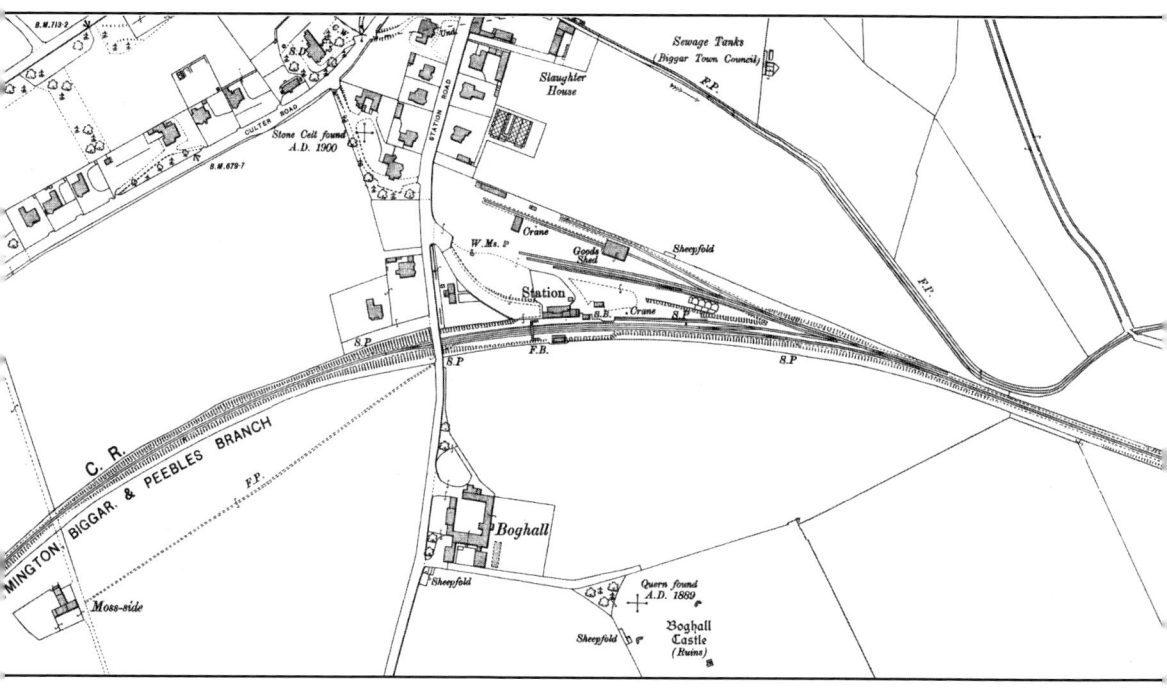

XXX. A 1909 map emphasises the curvature of the station here. Opened on 6th November 1860 it closed to passengers on 5th June 1950 although school traffic remained until 14th August of that year. The goods yard continued in use until 4th April 1966. The population in 1960 was 1,444.

90. The station entrance is seen here in the early days of the last century. A local delivery cart awaits the arrival of the next train. (J.Alsop coll.)

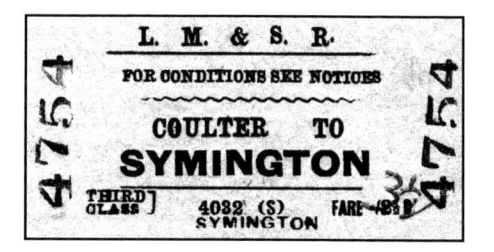

91. Looking towards Peebles on 1st June 1953. The goods yard is behind the signal box with the crane in the background being similar to the one in picture 97 at Broughton.
(C.J.B.Sanderson/ARPT)

92. The signal box and main station building are seen here after closure in August 1960.
(N.Forrest/Transport Treasury)

BIGGAR.

MARKET DAY.—Thursday.

FAIRS.—January, last Thursday, o.s.; March, 1st Thursday; April, last Thursday; August, last Thursday; October, last Thursday, o.s.

A small town situated in a hilly district, with a population of 2,000, and remarkable for its cattle fairs. The church, built by the Flemings, is in the form of a cross. Traces of a Roman camp may also be seen.

↑ Extract from *Bradshaws Guide*, 1866.

93. On 30th September 1961 the Branch Line Society ran the Pentland & Tinto Express which originated at Leith North. The headboard can be seen above the coupling hook. It visited a number of lines and was worked by McIntosh Class 19 0-4-4T no. 55124 throughout before returning to Edinburgh Waverley where the train terminated. Photo stops were provided at a number of stations including this one at Biggar. (N.Forrest/Transport Treasury)

94. The station remained relatively intact being used as part of a council yard when seen here on 20th October 1998. There were some short-lived plans for a heritage railway from Biggar to Broughton in the 1990s which came to nothing. The station building remains today although surrounded by housing and industrial buildings. Further planning consent was obtained early in 2023, which will see the trackbed breached by three houses. (G.W.Morrison)

BROUGHTON

XXXI. The station here served as a terminus when it opened on 6th November 1860. A temporary engine shed was provided here between 1860 and 1864 when it was replaced by a permanent structure at Peebles. The station lost its passenger services on 5th June 1950 but remained open for goods until 4th April 1966. The station also provided a short-lived passenger service during the construction of the Talla Reservoir.

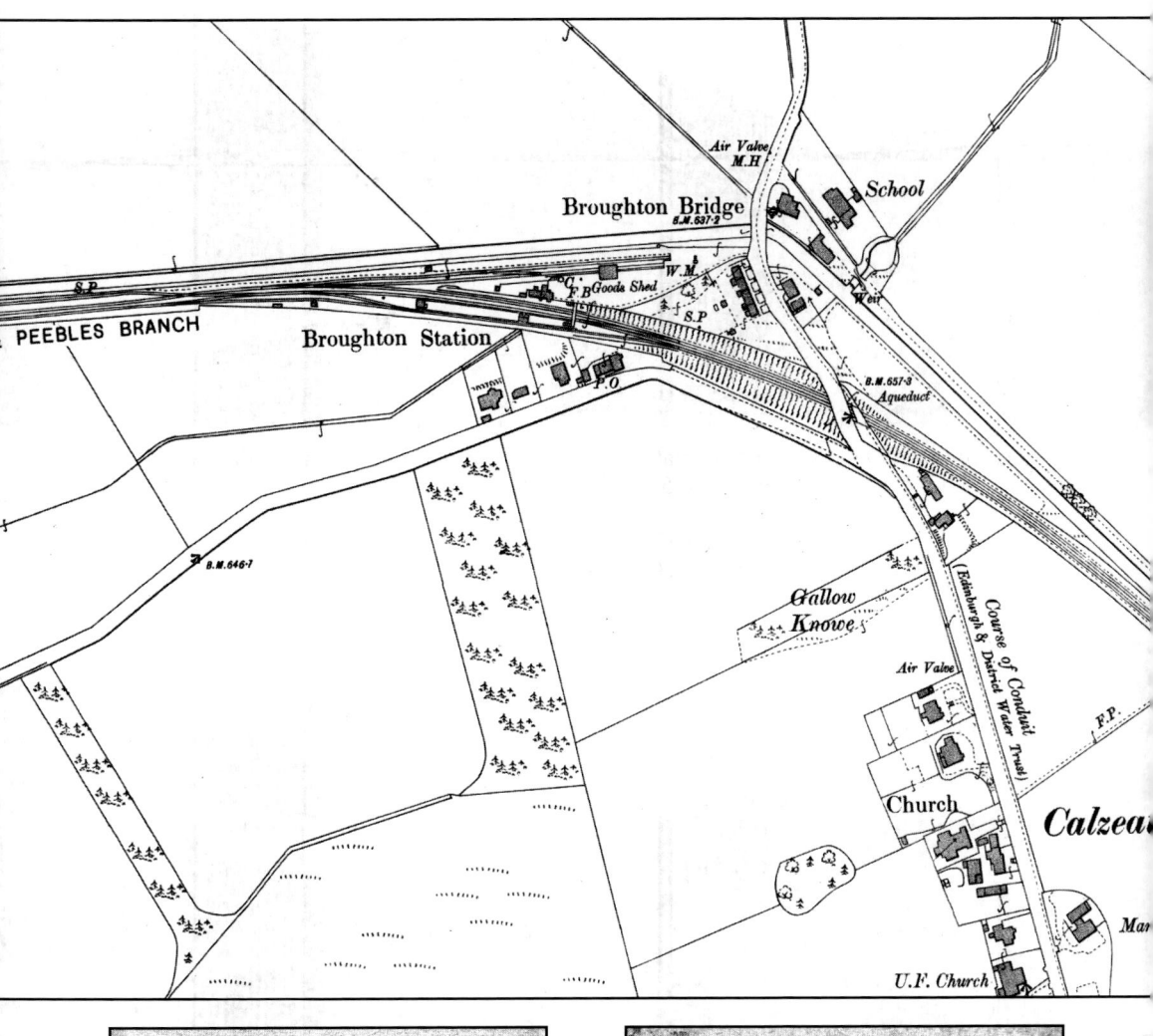

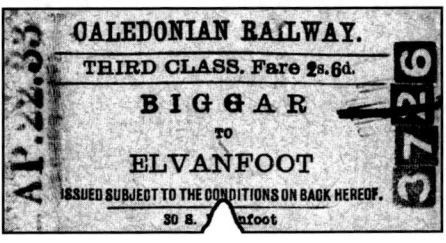

95. Looking west we see the island platform with the platform used by the works trains serving the Talla Railway, seen here around 1905, on the far left. (J.Alsop coll.)

96. Looking east around 1915 with the Talla line on the right removed. The station gardens have an impressive floral display showing. (J.Alsop coll.)

97. This rather unusual crane sitting on its own isolated section of track is seen here in August 1960 loading a container on to a Conflat wagon. The line remained open to serve the local abattoir, with the meat being transported to market in London and elsewhere on express freight trains. Note the XP (for express) markings on the Conflat wagon at the bottom of the picture. (N.Forrest/Transport Treasury)

98. The end of the line just beyond the station following the lifting of the route towards Peebles, which is seen here in August 1960. (N.Forrest/Transport Treasury)

The Talla Railway

XXXII. This was a temporary standard gauge line built by contractors building a reservoir for the Edinburgh & District Water Trust. In 1894, land was acquired in the valley of the Talla Water for the construction of a dam and reservoir. The Talla Water is a tributary of the River Tweed, which it joins at Tweedsmuir.

To build the reservoir, it was necessary to build a standard gauge line to transport the building materials to this otherwise remote spot.

In April 1895, the Water Trust reached agreement with the Caledonian Railway for the construction of an additional line from Broughton station to the junction of the private line which ran for some eight miles. Work on this line began on 28th September 1895 with the junction becoming Rachan Junction, a mile or so to the east of Broughton.

The line was officially opened on 29th September 1897 although the Caledonian had operated a special train to inspect the line in the March of that year. The line terminated at Victoria Lodge, which was built to accommodate the offices and works of the Water Trust.

Completion of the railway allowed the contractors to start building the reservoir. However, the main contractor, Young & Sons of Edinburgh were declared bankrupt in October 1899. A new contractor, John Best of Leith was appointed and Best soon built a halt opposite the Crook Inn that was a popular stopping place for the workers returning home on the workers trains to Broughton.

The reservoir was completed on 20th May 1905 and two special trains ran from Edinburgh to convey the guests.

Residents wanted the Caledonian Railway to take over the line and provide a regular service for residents. However, the area was sparsely populated and the company declined their requests. As a result, the line fell into disuse and, in 1910, a Glasgow contractor was tasked with removing the track. This was completed by 1912, although the trackbed can still be traced. (Middleton Press)

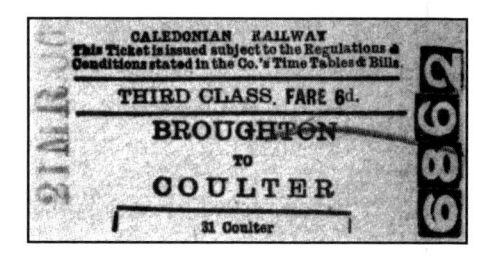

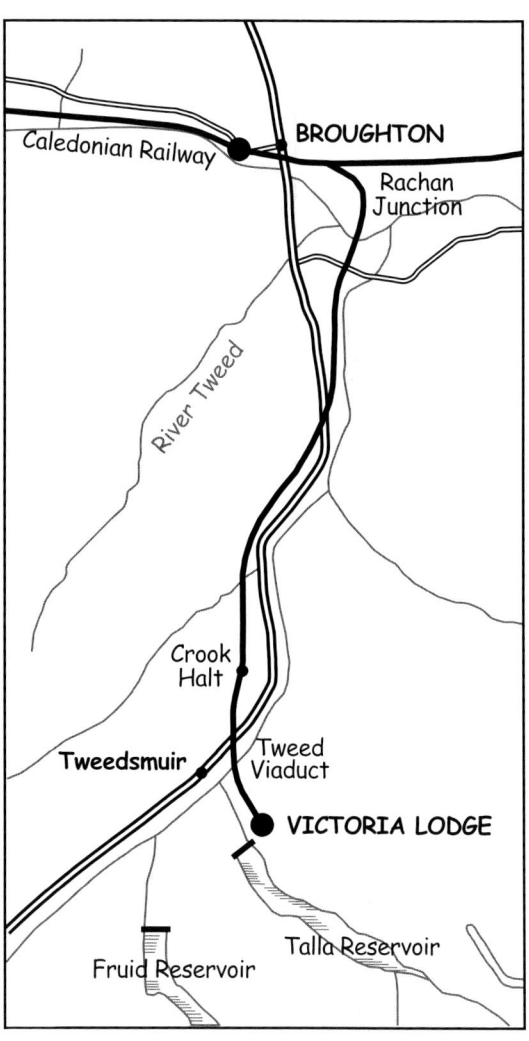

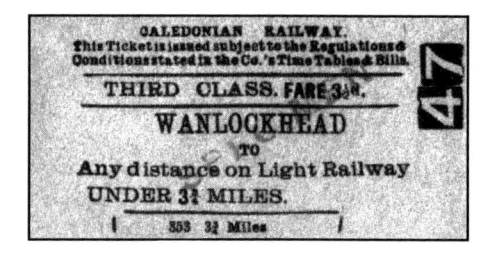

Crook Inn Halt

XXXIII. This 1908 6in map shows that the former Crook Inn has now been upgraded to a hotel.

The halt was provided here for workers to pay back some of their wages to the contractor John Best who owned the inn. Trains stopped here to allow them to partake of the beverages on offer between 1899 and 1905 when the work had been completed.

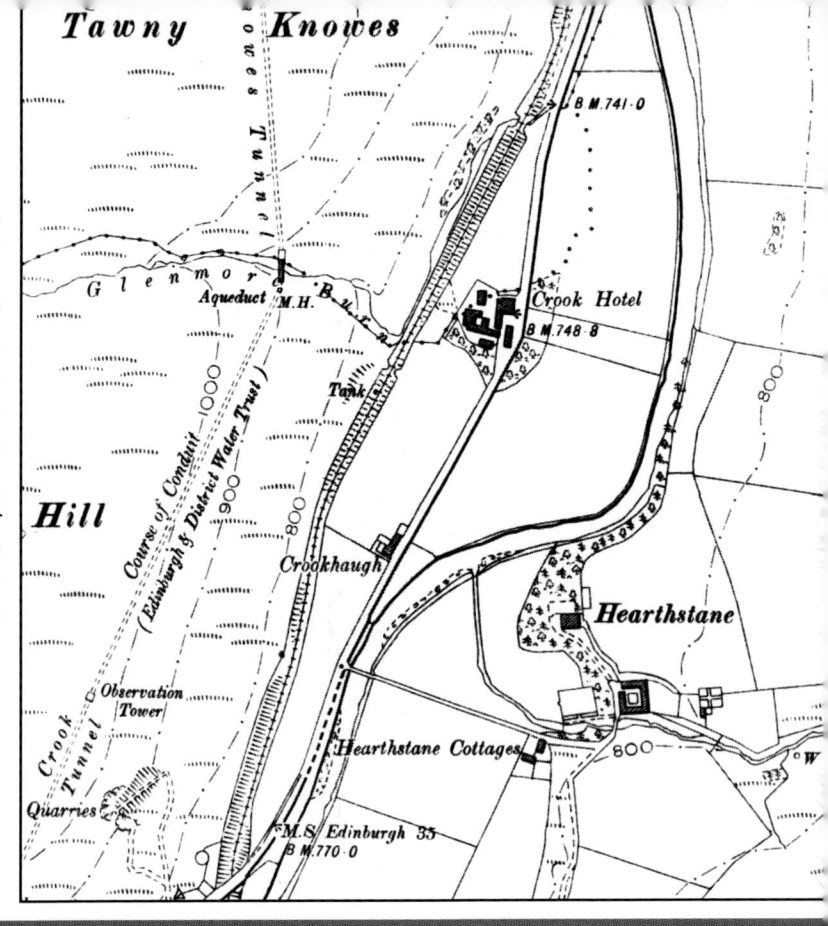

VICTORIA LODGE

99. At Victoria Lodge with one of the two special trains that were supplied by the Caledonian Railway so that dignitaries could attend the opening of the Talla Reservoir on 28th September 1905. Marquees have been erected alongside Victoria Lodge for the official opening by Lady Cranston. A further marquee has been supplied alongside the station.
(J.Alsop coll.)

XXXIV. Victoria Lodge was the nearest point to the head of the reservoir as shown on this 1909 6in map. The station opened in 1897 and closed in 1905.

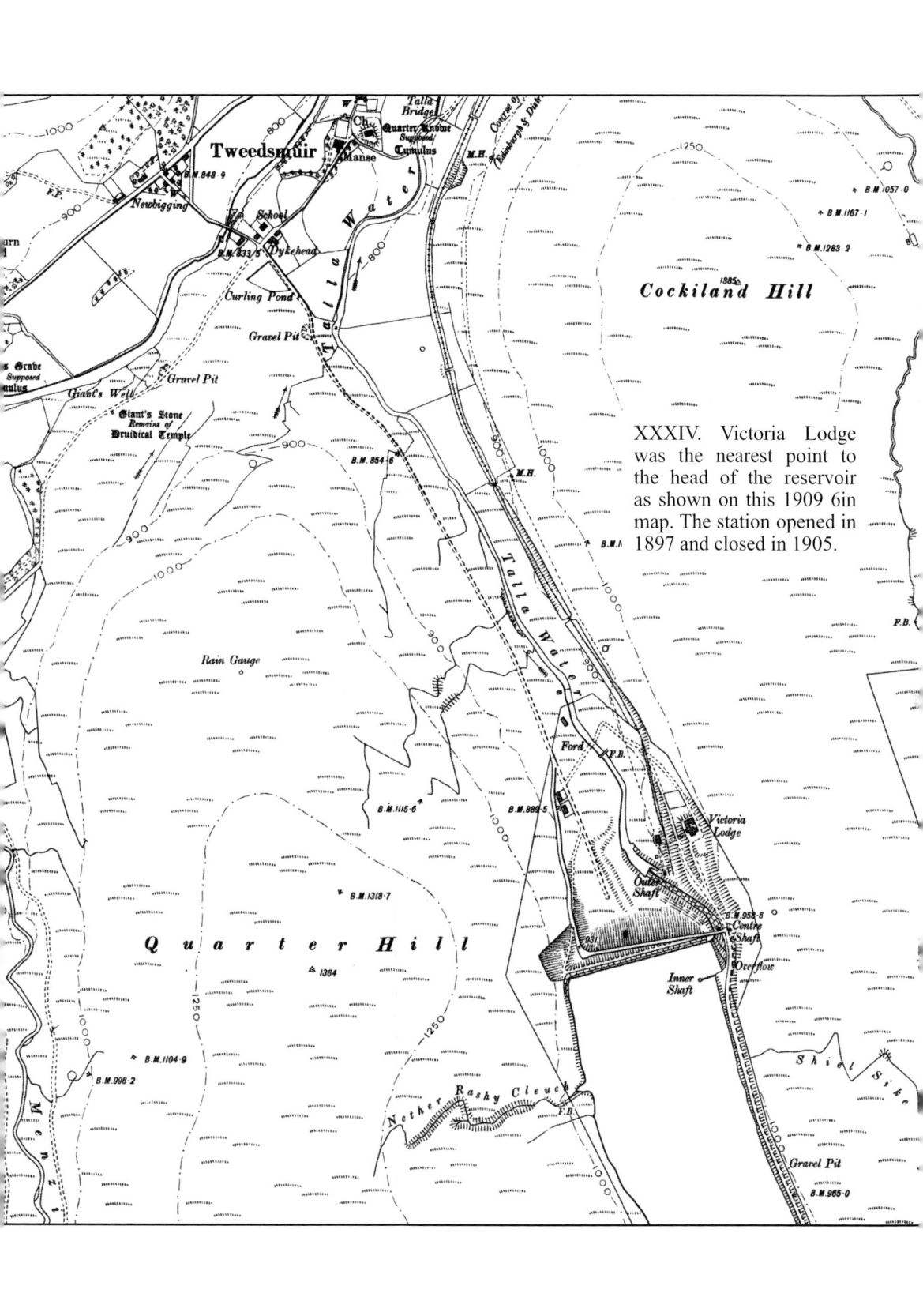

STOBO

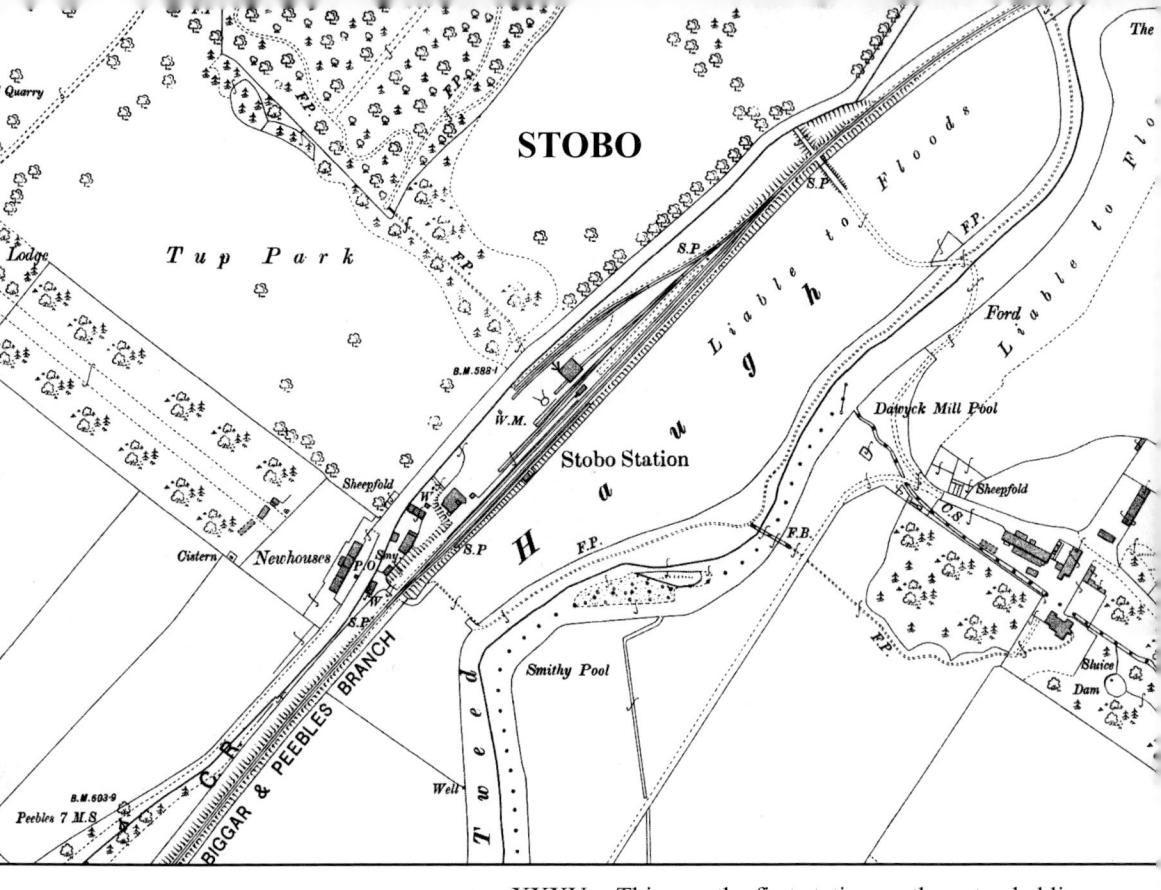

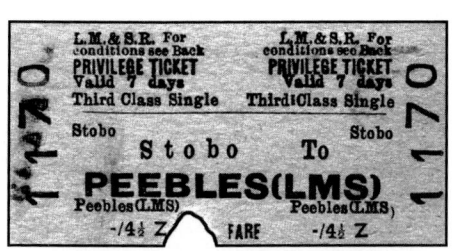

XXXV. This was the first station on the extended line to Peebles as seen here in 1908. The station opened on 1st February 1864. Passenger services were withdrawn on 5th June 1950 although goods services remained until 7th June 1954. The population in 1960 was just 237.

100. A commercial postcard dating around 1912 shows the platform-facing side of the station whilst the station staff look on. (LOSA)

101. A train awaits departure for Peebles around 1912. The second platform was added in 1906 and with it a 16-lever signal box. The box closed in 1921 and trains no longer crossed at Stobo, the line being worked as a single line between Broughton and Peebles. (LOSA)

LYNE

XXXVI. The station opened on 1st February 1864 as Lyne as marked on this 1908 map. In the 1922-23 edition of *Bradshaw*, it was noted that after 5pm it would be an unstaffed halt. It was renamed Lyne Halt between 1939 and 1948 before reverting to its former name in 1948. The station closed on 5th June 1950 but goods trains continued until 7th June 1954.

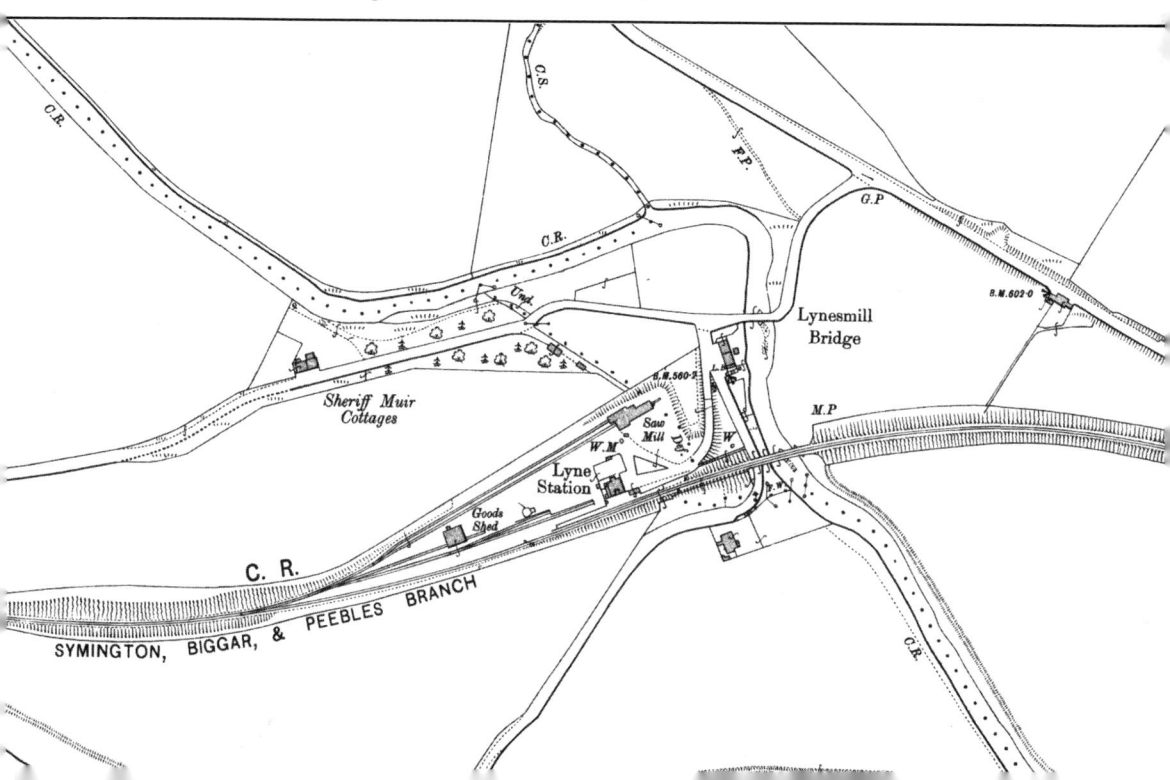

102. This view was taken in the 1930s looking towards Peebles. (LOSA)

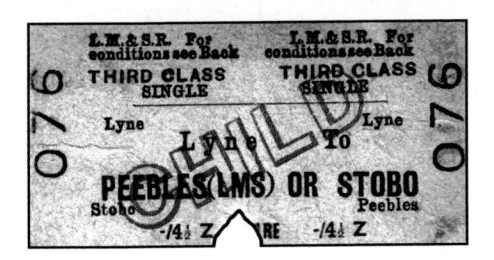

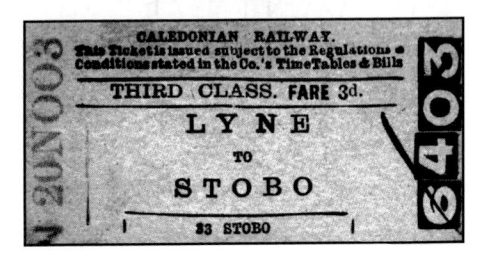

103. This view, taken on 1st June 1953, looks towards Symington three years after closure to passenger traffic. The weeds are beginning to take hold on the platform. (C.J.B.Sanderson/ARPT)

Peebles (CR) Shed

The shed here replaced the temporary one at Broughton when the line was extended to Peebles. The shed opened on 1st February 1864 and closed in 1940. Thereafter, locomotives for use on this line were provided by Carstairs shed. The location is shown on map XXXVII overleaf.

104. The engine shed was photographed on 19th June 1936 when still in daily use. It was at the Symington end of the platform with the bay platform to the right.
(W.A.Camwell/Stephenson Locomotive Society)

PEEBLES (CR)

105. A panoramic view taken in around 1912 showing part of the station building and the engine shed with the goods yard behind the coaches. The south bank of the River Tweed is in the foreground. (J.Alsop coll.)

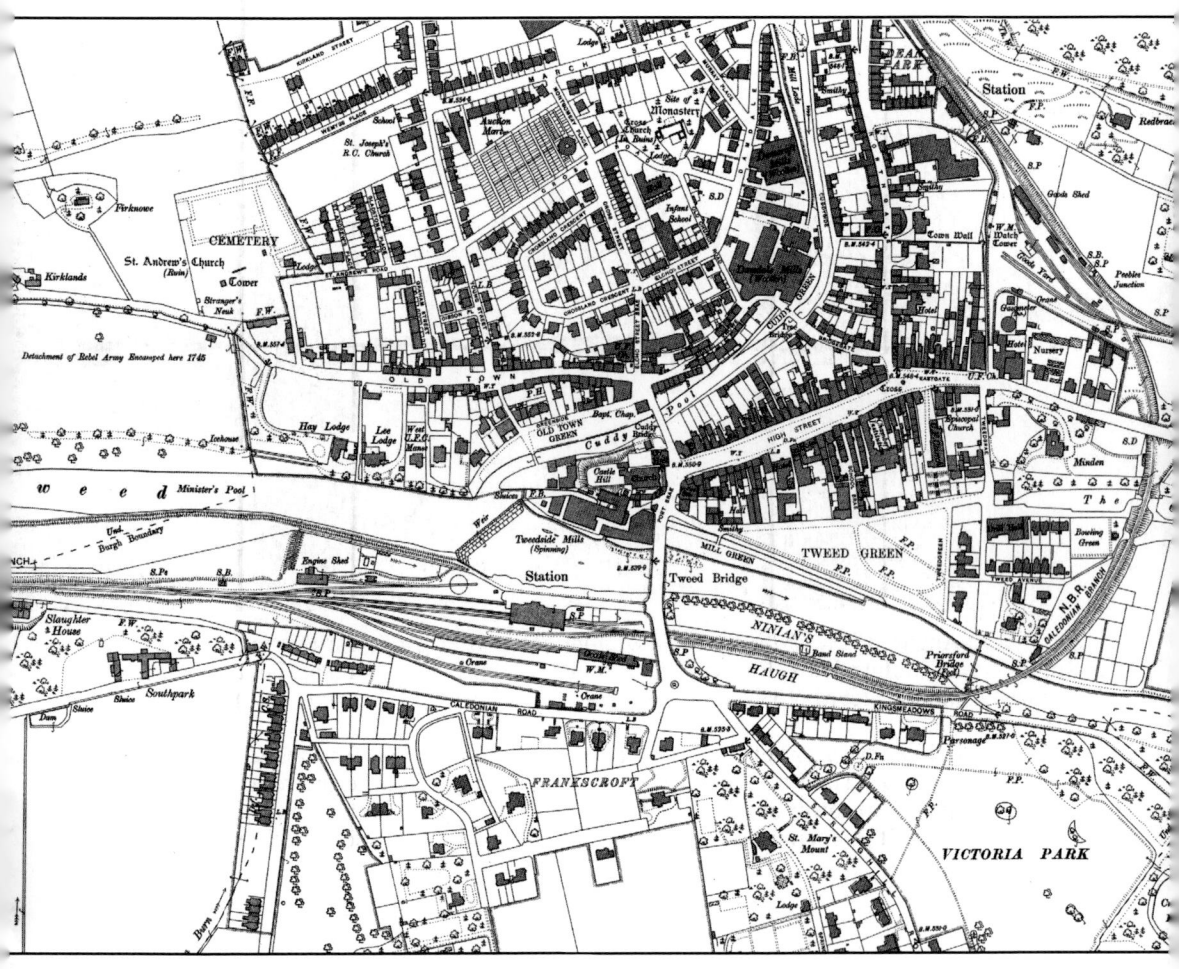

XXXVII. This 1908 map shows the station's location alongside the River Tweed. On the right-hand side can be seen the connecting line to join with the North British station, which was a requirement of the Act of Parliament that permitted construction of the extension from Broughton and the NBR line from Galashiels to Peebles via Innerleithen. Opened on 1st February 1864, it lost its passenger services on 5th June 1950. After closure of the line east of Broughton to all traffic, goods trains used the link to access the station, which was renamed Peebles West in September 1952 when continuing only as a goods station. Goods traffic was finally withdrawn on 1st August 1959. The former station site is now a housing estate. The population of Peebles was 5,662 in 1960 but had risen to 8,940 in the 2021 census.

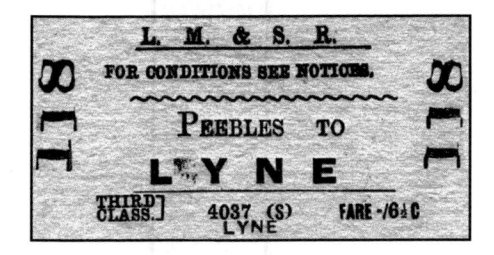

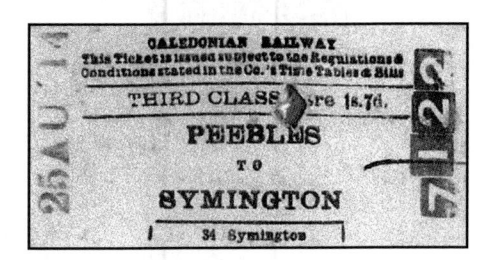

106. Dated August 1931, LMS liveried no. 17440 waits with a train for Symington. The locomotive is one of McIntosh's 711 class 0-6-0 locomotives nicknamed Jumbos, built in June 1896. It was withdrawn on 31st May 1950 from Stranraer shed. (J.Mann/A.E.Young coll.)

107. Taken in 1949, the year before closure, former LMS class 4P 4-4-0 no. 40903 with the name of its new owners 'BRITISH RAILWAYS' on the tender, is awaiting departure with a passenger train to Symington. The tower of Peebles Old Parish Church and a chimney from Castle Mill can be seen to the left of the locomotive. (W.A.Camwell/Stephenson Locomotive Society)

108. A 1950s view probably taken during the freight-only period. The coaching stock have SC (for Scottish Region) numbers on them. The Conflat wagons are carrying containers used for meat traffic. (N.E.Stead/Transport Treasury).

109. A view from 1st June 1953 taken from the station throat shows the island platform, overall roof and the goods yard off to the right. (C.J.B.Sanderson/ARPT)

110. The line that connected the two former stations in Peebles is now a footpath alongside the River Tweed, which is just off to the right. The bridge carries the B7062 road over the footpath with the former West station site visible through the bridge. Housing has now taken over most of the old station site but further developments were taking place behind the safety fencing when visited on 18th October 2022. (D.A.Lovett)

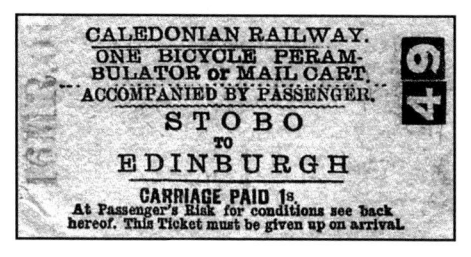

Peebles branch timetable for Summer 1947.

5. Carstairs to Dolphinton (CR)
BANKHEAD

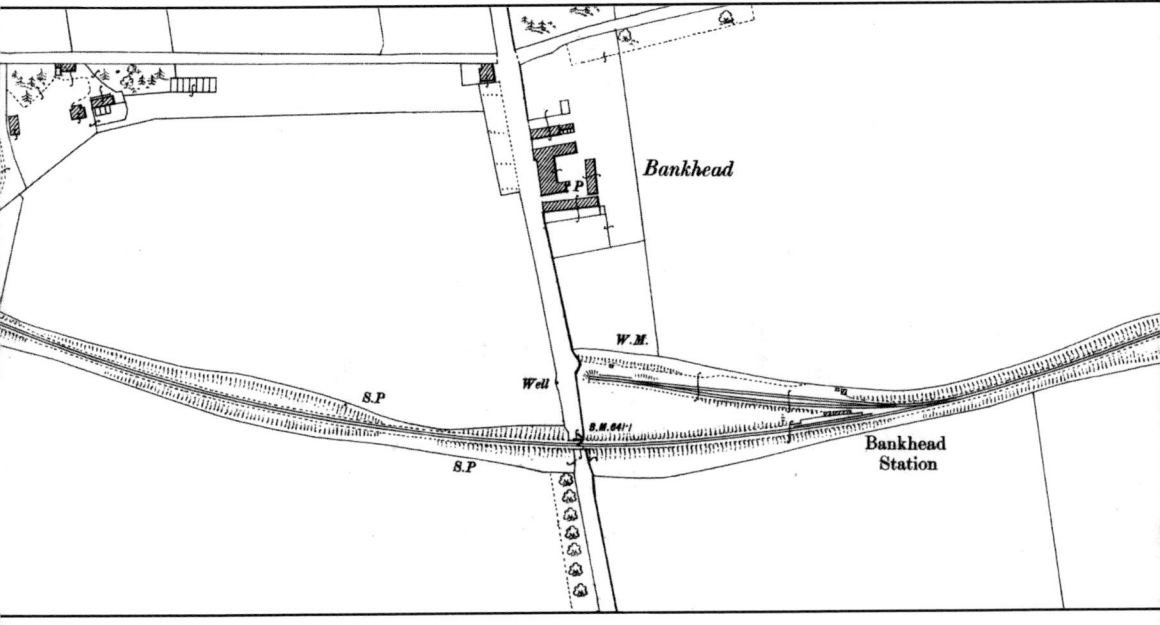

XXXVIII. Seen here in 1897, 30 years after it opened in November 1867, the station was temporarily closed between 12th September 1932 and 17th July 1933. It finally closed to passengers on 4th June 1945, although goods traffic was retained until 1st November 1950.

111. A 1930s view looking towards Dolphinton. Although it only had modest facilities, the station gardens and its well-kept appearance show the staff took great pride in their work. (LOSA)

NEWBIGGING

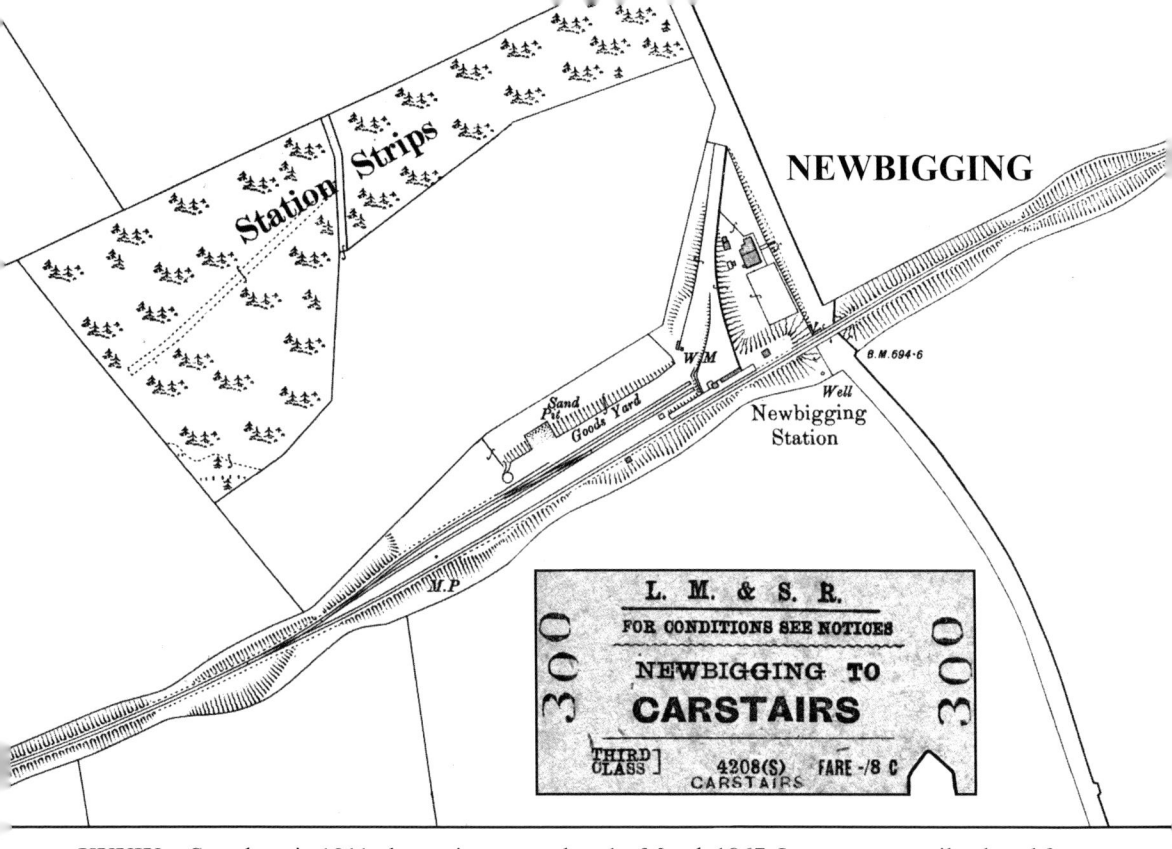

L. M. & S. R.
FOR CONDITIONS SEE NOTICES
NEWBIGGING TO **CARSTAIRS**
THIRD CLASS   4208(S)   FARE -/8 C
CARSTAIRS

XXXIX.   Seen here in 1911, the station opened on 1st March 1867. It was temporarily closed from 12th September 1932 until 17th July 1933. It closed to passengers permanently on 4th June 1945 and to goods on 1st November 1950.

112.   The station here has a more substantial stone-based platform than the wooden construction at Bankhead. In this 1930s view we are looking towards Dolphinton with the bridge carrying the line over the road just visible beyond the end of the platform. (LOSA)

113. The remains of the station are seen here on 3rd January 1976. The isolated location is emphasised by the light snowfall. (A.E.Young)

West Hall Milk Platform

XL. Located to the south of Westhall farm by a road overbridge, this 1910 6in map does not show the platform or any road access to it. We can only assume that the churns were manhandled to the platform from the bridge.

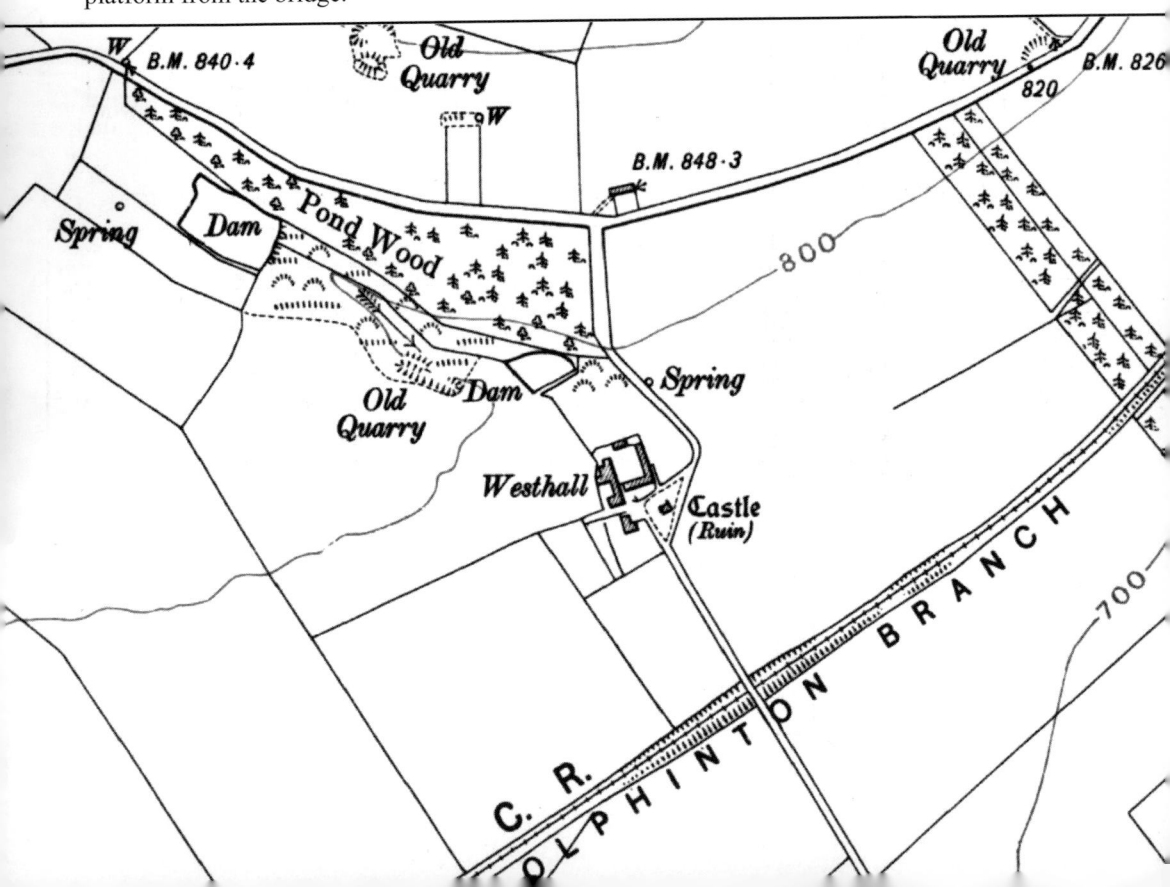

DUNSYRE

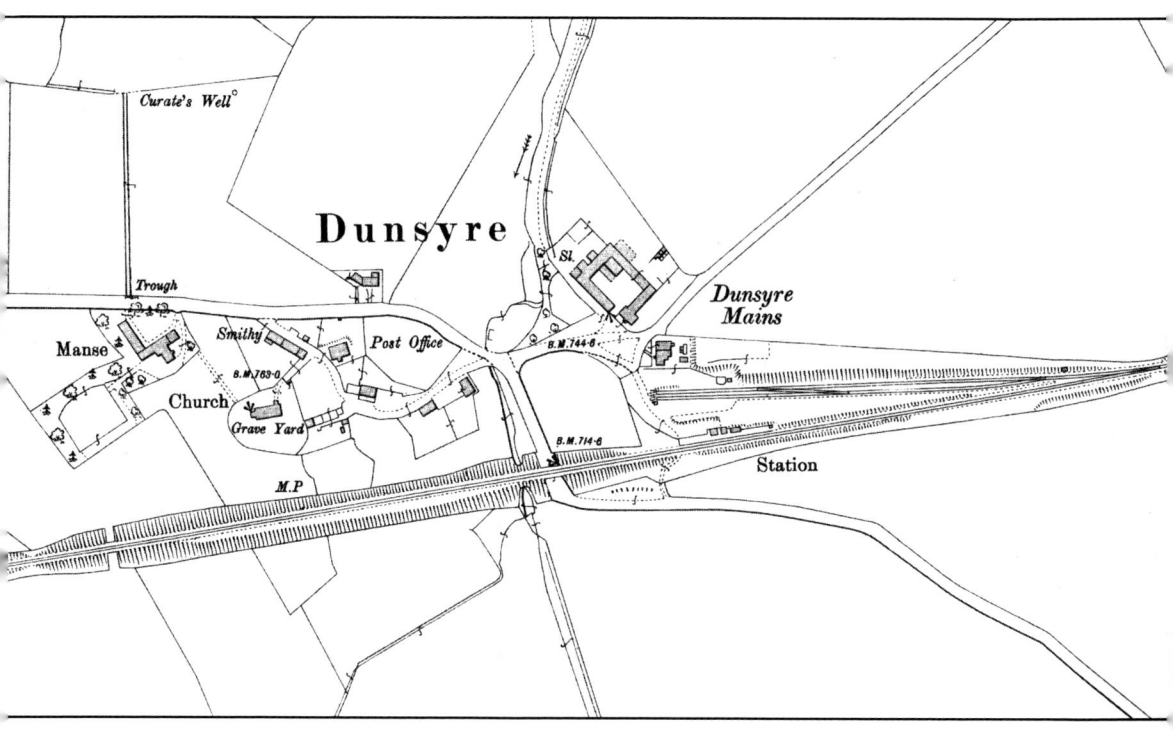

XLI. Seen here in 1910, the station was better placed to serve the local community. It opened on 1st March 1867 and, like the other intermediate stations on the branch, was closed between 12th September 1932 and 17th July 1933. Closure came on 4th June 1945 with goods following on 1st November 1950.

Timetable for Summer 1922, the last year of Caledonian Railway operation before the Grouping.

CARSTAIRS and DOLPHINTON.—Caledonian.

Miles from Carstairs		Week Days only.					Miles		Week Days only.			
		mrn	aft	aft					mrn	mrn	aft	
	831 Glasgow (Cen.) 842 dep	6 5	1 40	4F45	...	...		Dolphinton ....dep.	6 43	...	9 15	3 38
	837 Edinbro' (P. St.) ,,	6 30	12 50	4F40	...	...	2½	Dunsyre	6 49	...	9 21	3 44
	824 Carlisle .... ,,	5 23	12 51	3 31	...	...	6½	Newbigging	6 59	...	9 31	3 54
	Carstairs ....dep.	8 20	3 0	5 50	...	...	9	Bankhead..(837. S44, 859	7 5	...	9 37	4 0
2	Bankhead	8 25	3 5	5 55	...	...	11	Carstairs 824. 731. arr.	7 13	...	9 45	4 8
4½	Newbigging...........	8 31	3 11	6 2	...	...	8½	831 Carlisle .... arr.	11 5	...	12 52	6 50
8½	Dunsyre	8 41	3 21	6 13	...	...	38½	837 Edinbro' (P. St.) ,,	9 27	...	12 45	5 34
11	Dolphinton 789.....arr.	8 46	3 26	6 20	...	...	39¾	824 Glasgow (Cen.) 844 ,,	8 44	...	11 14	5 50

F Leaves at 4 10 aft. on Saturdays.   d Leaves Glasgow (Cen.) at 12 45 and Edinburgh (P. St.) at 2 aft. on Saturdays.

L. M. & S. R.
FOR CONDITIONS SEE NOTICES
Dunsyre TO
CARSTAIRS
THIRD CLASS   4209(S)   FARE 1/4 C
CARSTAIRS
0 50

114. Taken from an adjacent field, this view taken around 1912 shows the single platform and station buildings. A member of staff poses for the shot. (J.Alsop coll.)

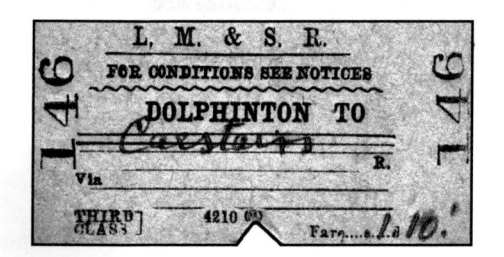

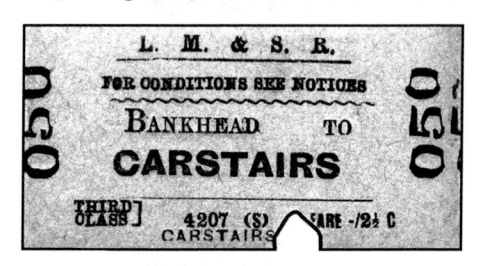

115. A 1930s view shows the well-kept gardens and spotless trackbed. (LOSA)

116. The station master stands proudly in front of his station in around 1910. It is likely that the lady and child are his wife and daughter. (LOSA)

Dolphinton Engine Shed

117. Taken from the site of the engine shed on 19th June 1936, the water tower remains with the former shed road providing access to it.

The 1910 map overleaf (XLII) shows the shed, far left. It was located west of the station and opened around 1868 when the former Dunblane shed building was transferred to Dolphinton for re-erection. It closed on 31st December 1915 although it was not until 1933 that the shed and turntable were removed. The Dolphinton branch locomotives were supplied from Carstairs shed thereafter. (W.A.Camwell/Stephenson Locomotive Society)

DOLPHINTON (CR)

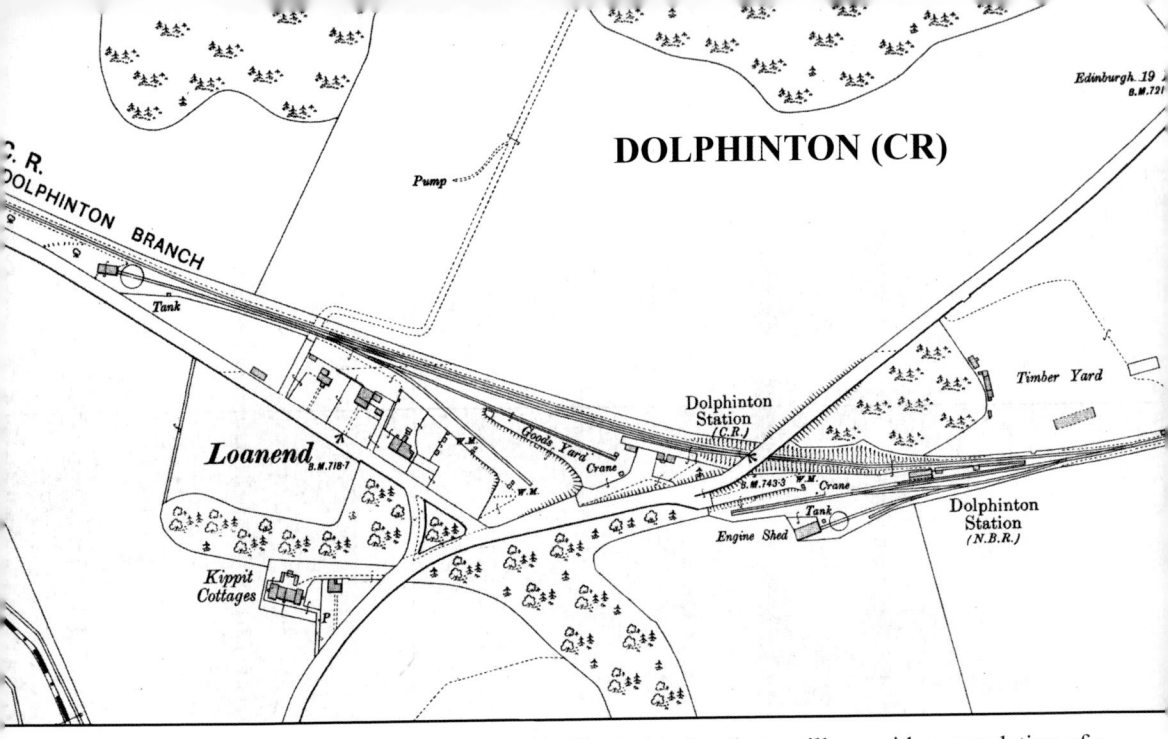

XLII. Seen here in 1910, it seems totally illogical today that a village with a population of a couple of hundred should be served by two railway companies, each with their own station. They were joined by a single line connection to allow transfer of goods between the two. The situation in Dolphinton arose because of the fierce rivalry between the two companies, which blocked any further extension on to each other's territory. The NBR station lost its passenger services as early as 1933, the CR station managed to survive until 1945.

The Caledonian station opened on 1st March 1867 and was closed temporarily between 12th September 1932 and 17th July 1933 when it reopened, with just one train a day being provided. Passenger services were withdrawn on 4th June 1945 with goods following on 1st November 1950. The population in 1960 was just 184.

118. Looking west we see the Caledonian station with the single line towards the rival North British facility continuing to the left of the picture. This dates from July 1909. (J.Alsop coll.)

119. Taken from the road bridge that separated the two stations, which were just 14 chains apart, this photo shows a train getting ready to depart for Carstairs in August 1912. (J.Alsop coll.)

120. A 1920s general view looking east shows a single platform, station building and road overbridge. The NBR station is visible through the arch of the bridge. (LOSA)

EVOLVING THE Vic Mitchell and Keith Smith ULTIMATE RAIL ENCYCLOPEDIA INTERNATIONAL

126a Camelsdale Road, GU27 3RJ. Tel:01730 813169

Our RAILWAY titles are listed below. Please check availability by looking at our website **www.middletonpress.co.uk**, telephoning us or by requesting a Brochure which includes our LATEST RAILWAY TITLES also our TRAMWAY, TROLLEYBUS, MILITARY and COASTAL series.

email:info@middletonpress.co.uk

A-978 0 906520 B- 978 1 873793 C- 978 1 901706 D-978 1 904473
E - 978 1 906008 F - 978 1 908174 G - 978 1 910356

A
- Abergavenny to Merthyr C 91 8
- Abertillery & Ebbw Vale Lines D 84 5
- Aberystwyth to Carmarthen E 90 1
- Alnmouth to Berwick G 50 0
- Alton - Branch Lines to A 11 6
- Ambergate to Buxton G 28 9
- Ambergate to Mansfield G 39 5
- Andover to Southampton A 82 6
- Ascot - Branch Lines around A 64 2
- Ashburton - Branch Line to B 95 4
- Ashford - Steam to Eurostar B 67 1
- Ashford to Dover A 48 2
- Austrian Narrow Gauge D 04 3
- Avonmouth - BL around D 42 5
- Aylesbury to Rugby D 91 3

B
- Baker Street to Uxbridge D 90 6
- Bala to Llandudno E 87 1
- Banbury to Birmingham D 27 2
- Banbury to Cheltenham E 63 5
- Bangor to Holyhead F 01 7
- Bangor to Portmadoc E 72 7
- Barking to Southend C 80 2
- Barmouth to Pwllheli E 53 6
- Barry - Branch Lines around D 50 0
- Bartlow - Branch Lines to F 27 7
- Basingstoke to Salisbury A 89 4
- Bath Green Park to Bristol C 36 9
- Bath to Evercreech Junction A 60 4
- Beamish 40 years on rails E94 9
- Beattock to Carstairs G 84 5
- Bedford to Wellingborough D 31 9
- Berwick to Drem F 64 2
- Berwick to St. Boswells F 75 8
- B'ham to Tamworth & Nuneaton F 63 5
- Birkenhead to West Kirby F 61 1
- Birmingham to Wolverhampton E253
- Blackburn to Hellifield F 95 6
- Bletchley to Cambridge D 94 4
- Bletchley to Rugby E 07 9
- Bodmin - Branch Lines around B 83 1
- Bolton to Preston G 61 6
- Boston to Lincoln F 80 2
- Bournemouth to Evercreech Jn A 46 8
- Bradshaw's History F18 5
- Bradshaw's Rail Times 1850 F 13 0
- Branch Lines series - see town names
- Brecon to Neath D 43 2
- Brecon to Newport D 16 6
- Brecon to Newtown E 06 2
- Brighton to Eastbourne A 16 1
- Brighton to Worthing A 03 1
- Bristol to Taunton D 03 6
- Bromley South to Rochester B 23 7
- Bromsgrove to Birmingham B 87 6
- Bromsgrove to Gloucester D 73 9
- Broxbourne to Cambridge F16 1
- Brunel - A railtour D 74 6
- Bude - Branch Line to B 29 9
- Burnham to Evercreech Jn B 68 0
- Buxton to Stockport G 32 6

C
- Cambridge to Ely D 55 5
- Canterbury - BLs around B 58 9
- Cardiff to Dowlais (Cae Harris) E 47 5
- Cardiff to Pontypridd E 95 6
- Cardiff to Swansea E 42 0
- Carlisle to Beattock G 69 2
- Carlisle to Hawick E 85 7
- Carmarthen to Fishguard E 66 6
- Caterham & Tattenham Corner B251
- Central & Southern Spain NG E 91 8
- Chard and Yeovil - BLs a C 30 7
- Charing Cross to Orpington A 96 3
- Cheddar - Branch Line to B 90 9
- Cheltenham to Andover C 43 7
- Cheltenham to Redditch D 81 4
- Chesterfield to Lincoln G 21 0
- Chester to Birkenhead F 21 5
- Chester to Manchester F 51 2
- Chester to Rhyl E 93 2
- Chester to Warrington F 40 6
- Chichester to Portsmouth A 14 7
- Clacton and Walton - BLs to F 04 8
- Clapham Jn to Beckenham Jn B 36 7
- Cleobury Mortimer - BLs a E 18 5
- Clevedon & Portishead - BLs to D180
- Consett to South Shields E 57 4
- Cornwall Narrow Gauge D 56 2
- Corris and Vale of Rheidol E 65 9
- Coventry to Leicester G 00 5
- Craven Arms to Llandeilo E 35 2
- Craven Arms to Wellington E 33 8
- Crawley to Littlehampton A 34 5
- Crewe to Manchester F 57 4
- Crewe to Wigan G 12 8
- Cromer - Branch Lines around C 26 0
- Cromford and High Peak G 35 7
- Croydon to East Grinstead B 48 0
- Crystal Palace & Catford Loop B 87 1
- Cyprus Narrow Gauge E 13 0

D
- Darjeeling Revisited F 09 3
- Darlington Leamside Newcastle E 28 4
- Darlington to Newcastle D 98 2
- Dartford to Sittingbourne B 34 3
- Denbigh - Branch Lines around F 32 1
- Derby to Chesterfield G 11 1
- Derby to Nottingham G 45 6
- Derby to Stoke-on-Trent F 93 2
- Derwent Valley - BL to the D 06 7
- Devon Narrow Gauge E 09 3
- Didcot to Banbury D 02 9
- Didcot to Swindon C 84 0
- Didcot to Winchester C 13 0
- Diss to Norwich G 22 7
- Dorset & Somerset NG D 76 0
- Douglas - Laxey - Ramsey E 75 8
- Douglas to Peel C 88 8
- Douglas to Port Erin C 55 0
- Douglas to Ramsey D 39 5
- Dover to Ramsgate A 78 9
- Drem to Edinburgh G 06 7
- Dublin Northwards in 1950s E 31 4
- Dunstable - Branch Lines to E 27 7

E
- Ealing to Slough C 42 0
- Eastbourne to Hastings A 27 7
- East Croydon to Three Bridges A 53 6
- Eastern Spain Narrow Gauge E 56 7
- East Grinstead - BLs to A 07 9
- East Kent Light Railway A 07 1
- East London - Branch Lines of C 44 4
- East London Line B 80 0
- East of Norwich - Branch Lines E 69 7
- Effingham Junction - BLs a A 74 1
- Ely to Norwich C 90 1
- Enfield Town & Palace Gates D 32 6
- Epsom to Horsham A 30 7
- Eritrean Narrow Gauge E 38 3
- Euston to Harrow & Wealdstone C 89 5
- Exeter to Barnstaple B 15 2
- Exeter to Newton Abbot C 49 9
- Exeter to Tavistock B 69 5
- Exmouth - Branch Lines to B 00 8

F
- Fairford - Branch Line to A 52 9
- Falmouth, Helston & St. Ives C 74 1
- Fareham to Salisbury A 67 3
- Faversham to Dover B 05 3
- Felixstowe & Aldeburgh - BL to D 20 3
- Fenchurch Street to Barking C 20 8
- Festiniog - 50 yrs of enterprise C 83 3
- Festiniog 1946-55 E 01 7
- Festiniog in the Fifties B 68 8
- Festiniog in the Sixties B 91 6
- Ffestiniog in Colour 1955-82 F 25 3
- Finsbury Park to Alexandra Pal C 02 8
- French Metre Gauge Survivors F 88 8
- Frome to Bristol B 77 0

G
- Gainsborough to Sheffield G 17 3
- Galashiels to Edinburgh F 52 9
- Gloucester to Bristol D 35 7
- Gloucester to Cardiff D 66 1
- Gosport - Branch Lines around A 36 9
- Greece Narrow Gauge D 72 2
- Guildford to Redhill A 63 5

H
- Hampshire Narrow Gauge D 36 4
- Harrow to Watford D 14 2
- Harwich & Hadleigh - BLs to F 02 4
- Harz Revisited F 62 8
- Hastings to Ashford A 37 6
- Hawick to Galashiels F 36 9
- Hawkhurst - Branch Line to A 66 6
- Hayling - Branch Line to A 12 3
- Hay-on-Wye - BL around D 92 0
- Haywards Heath to Seaford A 28 4
- Hemel Hempstead - BLs to D 88 3
- Henley, Windsor & Marlow - BLa C77 2
- Hereford to Newport D 54 8
- Hertford & Hatfield - BLs a E 58 1
- Hertford Loop E 71 0
- Hexham to Carlisle D 75 3
- Hexham to Hawick F 08 6
- Hitchin to Peterborough D 07 4
- Horsham - Branch Lines to A 02 4
- Hull, Hornsea and Withernsea G 27 2
- Hull to Scarborough G 60 9
- Huntingdon - Branch Line to A 93 2

I
- Ilford to Shenfield C 97 0
- Ilfracombe - Branch Line to B 21 3
- Ilkeston to Chesterfield G 26 5
- Inverkeithing to Thornton Jct G 76 0
- Ipswich to Diss F 81 9
- Ipswich to Saxmundham C 41 3
- Isle of Man Railway Journey F 94 9
- Isle of Wight Lines - 50 yrs C 12 3
- Italy Narrow Gauge F 17 8

K
- Kent Narrow Gauge C 45 1
- Kettering to Nottingham F 82-6
- Kidderminster to Shrewsbury E 10 9
- Kingsbridge - Branch Line to C 98 7
- Kings Cross to Potters Bar E 62 8
- King's Lynn to Hunstanton F 58 1
- Kingston & Hounslow Loops A 83 3
- Kingswear - Branch Line to C 17 8

L
- Lambourn - Branch Line to C 70 3
- Lancaster to Oxenholme G 77 7
- Launceston & Princetown - BLs C 19 2
- Leeds to Selby G 47 0
- Leek - Branch Line From G 01 2
- Leicester to Burton F 85 7
- Leicester to Nottingham G 15 9
- Lewisham to Dartford A 92 5
- Lincoln to Cleethorpes F 56 7
- Lincoln to Doncaster G 62 3
- Lines around Newmarket G 54 8
- Lines around Stamford F 98 7
- Lines around Wimbledon B 75 6
- Lines North of Stoke G 29 6
- Liverpool to Runcorn G 72 2
- Liverpool Street to Chingford D 01 2
- Liverpool Street to Ilford C 34 5
- Llandeilo to Swansea E 46 8
- London Bridge to Addiscombe B 20 6
- London Bridge to East Croydon A 58 1
- Longmoor - Branch Lines to A 41 3
- Looe - Branch Line to C 22 2
- Loughborough to Ilkeston G 24 1
- Loughborough to Nottingham F 68 0
- Lowestoft - BLs around E 40 6
- Ludlow to Hereford E 14 7
- Lydney - Branch Lines around E 26 0
- Lyme Regis - Branch Line to A 45 1
- Lynton - Branch Line to B 04 6

M
- Machynlleth to Barmouth E 54 3
- Maesteg and Tondu Lines F 06 2
- Majorca & Corsica Narrow Gauge F 41 3
- Manchester to Bacup G 46 3
- Mansfield to Doncaster G 23 4
- March - Branch Lines around B 09 1
- Market Drayton - BLs around F 67 3
- Market Harborough to Newark F 86 4
- Marylebone to Rickmansworth D 49 4
- Melton Constable to Yarmouth Bch E031
- Midhurst - Branch Lines of E 78 9
- Midhurst - Branch Lines of F 00 0
- Minehead - Branch Line to A 80 2
- Monmouth - Branch Lines to E 20 8
- Monmouthshire Eastern Valleys D 71 5
- Moretonhampstead - BL to C 27 7
- Moreton-in-Marsh to Worcester D 26 5
- Morpeth to Bellingham F 87 1
- Mountain Ash to Neath D 80 7

N
- Newark to Doncaster F 78 9
- Newbury to Westbury C 66 6

- Newcastle to Alnmouth G 36 4
- Newcastle to Hexham D 69 2
- Newmarket to Haughley & Laxfield G 71 5
- New Mills to Sheffield G 44 9
- Newport (IOW) - Branch Lines to A 26 0
- Newquay - Branch Lines to C 71 0
- Newton Abbot to Plymouth C 60 4
- Newtown to Aberystwyth E 41 3
- Northampton to Peterborough F 92 5
- North East German NG D 44 9
- Northern Alpine Narrow Gauge F 37 6
- Northern Spain Narrow Gauge E 83 3
- North London Line B 94 7
- North of Birmingham F 55 0
- North of Grimsby - Branch Lines G 09 8
- North Woolwich - BLs around C 65 9
- Nottingham to Boston F 70 3
- Nottingham to Kirkby Bentinck G 38 8
- Nottingham to Lincoln F 43 7
- Nottingham to Mansfield G 52 4
- Nuneaton to Loughborough G 08 1

O
- Ongar - Branch Line to E 05 5
- Orpington to Tonbridge B 03 9
- Oswestry - Branch Lines around E 60 4
- Oswestry to Whitchurch E 81 9
- Oxford to Bletchley D 57 9
- Oxford to Moreton-in-Marsh D 15 9

P
- Paddington to Ealing C 37 6
- Paddington to Princes Risborough C819
- Padstow - Branch Line to B 54 1
- Peebles Loop G 19 7
- Pembroke and Cardigan - BLs to F 29 1
- Peterborough to Kings Lynn E 32 1
- Peterborough to Lincoln F 89 5
- Peterborough to Newark F 72 7
- Plymouth - BLs around B 98 5
- Plymouth to St. Austell C 63 5
- Pontypool to Mountain Ash D 65 4
- Pontypridd to Merthyr F 14 7
- Pontypridd to Port Talbot E 86 4
- Porthmadog 1954-94 - BLa B 31 2
- Portmadoc 1923-46 - BLa B 13 8
- Portsmouth to Southampton A 31 4
- Portugal Narrow Gauge E 67 3
- Potters Bar to Cambridge D 70 8
- Preston to Blackpool G 16 6
- Preston to the Fylde Coast G 81 4
- Preston to Lancaster G 74 6
- Princes Risborough - BL to D 05 0
- Princes Risborough to Banbury C 85 7

R
- Railways to Victory C 16 1
- Reading to Basingstoke B 27 5
- Reading to Didcot C 79 6
- Reading to Guildford A 47 5
- Redhill to Ashford A 73 4
- Return to Blaenau 1970-82 C 64 2
- Rhyl to Bangor F 15 4
- Rhymney & New Tredegar Lines E 48 2
- Rickmansworth to Aylesbury D 61 6
- Romania & Bulgaria NG E 23 9
- Ross-on-Wye - BLs around E 30 7
- Ruabon to Barmouth E 84 0
- Rugby to Birmingham E 37 6
- Rugby to Loughborough F 12 3
- Rugby to Stafford F 07 9
- Rugeley to Stoke-on-Trent F 90 1
- Ryde to Ventnor A 19 2

S
- Salisbury to Westbury B 39 8
- Salisbury to Yeovil B 06 0
- Sardinia and Sicily Narrow Gauge F 50 5
- Saxmundham to Yarmouth C 69 7
- Saxony & Baltic Germany Revisited F 71 0
- Saxony Narrow Gauge D 47 0
- Scunthorpe to Doncaster G 34 0
- Seaton & Sidmouth - BLs to A 95 6
- Selsey - Branch Line to A 04 8
- Sheerness - Branch Line to B 16 2
- Sheffield towards Manchester G 18 0
- Shenfield to Ipswich F 96 3
- Shildon to Stockton G 79 1
- Shrewsbury - Branch Line to A 86 4
- Shrewsbury to Chester E 70 3
- Shrewsbury to Crewe F 48 2
- Shrewsbury to Ludlow E 29 1
- Shrewsbury to Newtown E 29 1
- Sirhowy Valley Line E 72 2
- Sittingbourne to Ramsgate A 90 1
- Skegness & Mablethorpe - BL to F 84 0
- Slough to Newbury C 56 7
- South African Two-foot gauge E 51 2
- Southampton to Bournemouth A 42 0
- Southend & Southminster BLs E 76 5
- Southern Alpine Narrow Gauge F 22 2

- South London Line B 46 6
- South Lynn to Norwich City F 03 1
- Southwold - Branch Line to A 15 4
- Spalding - Branch Lines around E 52 6
- Spalding to Grimsby F 65 9 6
- Stafford to Chester F 34 5
- Stafford to Wellington F 59 8
- St Albans to Bedford D 08 1
- St. Austell to Penzance C 67 3
- St. Boswell to Berwick F 44 4
- Stourbridge to Wolverhampton E 16 1
- St. Pancras to Barking D 68 5
- St. Pancras to Folkestone E 88 8
- St. Pancras to St. Albans C 78 9
- Stratford to Cheshunt F 53 6
- Stratford-u-Avon to Birmingham D 77
- Stratford-u-Avon to Cheltenham C 25
- Sudbury - Branch Lines to F 19 2
- Surrey Narrow Gauge C 87 1
- Sussex Narrow Gauge C 68 0
- Swaffham - Branch Lines around F 97
- Swanage to 1999 - BL to A 33 8
- Swanley to Ashford B 45 9
- Swansea - Branch Lines around F 38
- Swansea to Carmarthen E 59 8
- Swindon to Bristol C 96 3
- Swindon to Gloucester D 46 3
- Swindon to Newport D 30 2
- Swiss Narrow Gauge C 94 9

T
- Talyllyn 60 E 98 7
- Tamworth to Derby F 76 5
- Taunton to Barnstaple B 60 2
- Taunton to Exeter C 82 6
- Taunton to Minehead F 94 9
- Tavistock to Plymouth B 88 6
- Tenterden - Branch Line to A 21 5
- Three Bridges to Brighton A 35 2
- Tilbury Loop C 86 4
- Tiverton - BLs around C 62 8
- Tivetshall to Beccles D 41 8
- Tonbridge to Hastings A 44 4
- Torrington - Branch Lines to B 37 4
- Tourist Railways of France G 04 3
- Towcester - BLs around E 39 0
- Tunbridge Wells BLs A 32 1

U
- Upwell - Branch Line to B 64 0
- Uttoxeter to Macclesfield G 05 0
- Uttoxeter to Buxton G 33 3

V
- Victoria to Bromley South A 98 7
- Victoria to East Croydon A 40 6
- Vivarais Revisited E 08 6

W
- Walsall Routes F 45 1
- Wantage - Branch Line to D 25 8
- Wareham to Swanage 50 yrs D 09 8
- Watercress Line G 75 3
- Waterloo to Windsor A 54 3
- Waterloo to Woking A 38 3
- Watford to Leighton Buzzard D 45 6
- Wellingborough to Leicester F 73 4
- Welshpool to Llanfair E 49 9
- Wenford Bridge to Fowey C 09 3
- Wennington to Morecambe G 58 6
- Westbury to Bath B 55 8
- Westbury to Taunton C 76 5
- West Cornwall Mineral Rlys D 47 7
- West Croydon to Epsom B 08 4
- West German Narrow Gauge D 93 7
- West London - BLs of C 50 5
- West London Line B 84 8
- West Somerset Railway G 78 4
- West Wiltshire - BLs of D 12 8
- Weymouth - BLs A 65 9
- Willesden Jn to Richmond B 71 8
- Wimbledon to Beckenham C 58 1
- Wimbledon to Epsom B 62 6
- Wimborne - BLs around A 97 0
- Wirksworth - Branch Lines to C 14
- Wisbech - BLs around C 01 7
- Witham & Kelvedon - BLs a E 82 6
- Woking to Alton A 59 8
- Woking to Portsmouth A 25 3
- Woking to Southampton A 55 0
- Wolverhampton to Shrewsbury C 14
- Wolverhampton to Stafford F 79 6
- Worcester to Birmingham D 97 5
- Worcester to Hereford D 38 8
- Worthing to Chichester A 06 2
- Wrexham to New Brighton F 47 5
- Wroxham - BLs around F 31 4

Y
- Yeovil - 50 yrs change C 38 3
- Yeovil to Dorchester A 76 5
- Yeovil to Exeter A 91 8
- York to Scarborough F 23 9